Urban Planning Today

HARVARD DESIGN MAGAZINE READERS

William S. Saunders, Editor

1. Commodification and Spectacle in Architecture
2. Sprawl and Suburbia
3. Urban Planning Today

Urban Planning Today

A Harvard Design Magazine Reader

Introduction by Alexander Garvin

William S. Saunders, Editor

University of Minnesota Press | Minneapolis | London

These essays were previously published in *Harvard Design Magazine*, Harvard University Graduate School of Design; Peter G. Rowe, Dean, 1992–2004; Alan Altshuler, Dean, 2005–.

Thanks to coordinator Meghan Ryan for her work on *Harvard Design Magazine* and this book.

Published by the University of Minnesota Press
111 Third Avenue South, Suite 290
Minneapolis, MN 55401-2520
http://www.upress.umn.edu

Library of Congress Cataloging-in-Publication Data

Urban planning today : a Harvard Design Magazine reader / introduction by Alexander Garvin ; William S. Saunders, editor.
p. cm. — (Harvard Design Magazine Readers ; 3)
Includes bibliographical references and index.
ISBN-13: 978-0-8166-4756-9 (hc : alk. paper)
ISBN-10: 0-8166-4756-9 (hc : alk. paper)
ISBN-13: 978-0-8166-4757-6 (pb : alk. paper)
ISBN-10: 0-8166-4757-7 (pb : alk. paper)
1. City planning. 2. City planning—Case studies. I. Saunders, William S. II. Series.
HT166.U7433 2006
307.1'216—dc22

2006008722

Printed in the United States of America on acid-free paper

The University of Minnesota is an equal-opportunity educator and employer.

12 11 10 09 08 07 06 10 9 8 7 6 5 4 3 2 1

Contents

vii Preface **William S. Saunders**

xi Introduction: Planning Now for the Twenty-first Century **Alexander Garvin**

1 1. The Return of Urban Renewal: Dan Doctoroff's Grand Plans for New York City **Susan S. Fainstein**

14 2. Deadlock Plus 50: On Public Housing in New York **Richard Plunz and Michael Sheridan**

24 3. Democracy Takes Command: The New Community Planning and the Challenge to Urban Design **John Kaliski**

38 4. Can Planning Be a Means to Better Architecture? Chicago's Building Boom and Design Quality **Lynn Becker**

48 5. An Anatomy of Civic Ambition in Vancouver: Toward Humane Density **Leonie Sandercock**

63 6. Paved with Good Intentions: Boston's Central Artery Project and a Failure of City Building **Hubert Murray**

83 7. Public Planning and Private Initiative: The South Boston Waterfront **Matthew J. Kiefer**

93 8. Omaha by Design—All of It: New Prospects in Urban Planning and Design **Jonathan Barnett**

106 9. Is Eminent Domain for Economic Development Constitutional? **Jerold S. Kayden**

117 10. From New Regionalism to the Urban Network: Changing the Paradigm of Growth **Peter Calthorpe**

131 11. Design by Deception: The Politics of Megaproject Approval **Bent Flyvbjerg**

149 Contributors

Preface

William S. Saunders

This volume is the third in a series addressing urgent contemporary issues in design and the built environment. The diverse and often conflicting perspectives presented in these essays will allow readers to understand the significant concerns and points of debate. The assumption is not that all positions articulated here are equally "right," but that one needs to understand the ways in which reasonable people can disagree to clarify one's own thinking about these issues.

The essays here were selected from the pages of *Harvard Design Magazine*, primarily its Spring/Summer 2005 issue. They are reappearing in this book relatively soon because they are particularly timely—directed at the realities of the middle of the first decade of the twenty-first century—and because this issue, under great demand, quickly sold out.

Urban planning now, at least in the United States, raises a few hard questions: What works better, top-down or bottom-up control? regulated or unfettered design?

If first you imagine yourself in Portland, Oregon, waiting for a light-rail vehicle and surrounded by street trees, benches, five-story brick buildings, and nearby open storefronts, and then you imagine yourself in Chicago's new Millennium Park, looking up at Anish Kapoor's dazzling steel bean and aware of street traffic and high-rises at your back, you may get a sense of one planning trade-off. Portland is oh so gentle and kind, oh so civilized and comfortable—yet one can easily feel understimulated, even sedated, there. Downtown Chicago, particularly at its new park, is a jolt, almost overstimulating, more wow than workaday.

Perhaps cities need to offer both kinds of experiences, but at the moment it would seem that most planners, for various good reasons, are working for the Portland model. Of course neither model predominates in America, and the one that does—single-use zoning and free-market development geared toward economic growth—has created problems planners have long recognized and the general public is recently getting more into focus: auto-dependency, long commutes, visual pollution, boredom and social isolation, expensive public infrastructure, needless destruction of the countryside, and so on. The wholly reasonable response (to make and support a multicentered, mixed-use, dense, transit-supported, walkable, self-sufficient "village" settlement pattern for cities, suburbia, and the countryside) has become a given among planners, architects, and landscape architects and a steadily growing but still minority choice for developers and consumers.

The essays in this book evoke two fundamental questions about this "Portland" model: Is it a pipe dream in an auto-addicted society, and does it reduce urbanity to a dull lowest common denominator? The sole exemplary large-scale environment depicted here is Vancouver, Canada, in which dense high-rise living has been humanized by street-level vibrant public life (with local stores, parks, and row houses fronting the towers). The U.S. models presented are almost entirely as yet unrealized, and one is unsure how much of a difference their realization (which may or may not be widely possible) could make. (Planners sometimes cite public survey preferences for models of denser new urbanism but admit that individual consumers keep buying detached houses—perhaps their only affordable option.) The sheer presence of lots of people on the streets may make Vancouver a vibrant place, but the images of its streets show no hint of the design vitality of Chicago's lakefront.

This leads us to the second dilemma/trade-off central in the essays here: Which distribution of power—top-down or bottom-up—is most likely to lead to positive urbanity? The implications of the Chicago and the Boston contemporary cases are that extraordinary achievement is most often the result of charismatic or forceful leadership by the Daleys, Burnhams, Mieses, and Olmsteds of this world, and that diffusion of power can lead to inertia and/or mediocre achievement.

Yet, like the support of denser mixed-use settlements, the support of significant public influence in (if not leadership of) the planning process is now almost a given, even if the result is some amount of dumbing down. Although the higher courts have yet to establish clear national guidelines about the use of eminent domain to enable development (is seizing private property OK to fulfill a general and important public need but not to promote finite job and business tax revenue growth?), nothing like the bulldozing of Boston's West End in 1959 will occur in our lifetimes.

The writers here all oppose city making in the hands of a bullying few but focus differently on the mixed bag of results from power in the hands of "the people" or of government bureaucrats. In Los Angeles, it seems that major projects have become more enlightened and urbane because of public participation. In Chicago, public establishment of baseline design rules for residential high-rises has seemingly led to some banal and phony architecture. In Boston, public exactions on private development have stalled urbanistically worthy projects, whereas in Vancouver they have helped positive development flourish. Fortunately, it seems as though the proportion of civic-minded, informed citizens is increasing relative to the proportion of self-centered and ill-informed NIMBYs.

So where are planners left in these trade-offs? Expert assistants who ensure broader views and offer alluring alternatives to the public? Certainly. Promoters of structural (not merely "decorative") changes in settlement patterns that create more sustainable ways of living? One would hope. Promoters of occasional exceptions to rules in order to find a place for the authentic, the extraordinary, the unprecedented, the inspired, and the unplanable? For this we need planners' mercurial cousins, the designers.

Introduction

Planning Now for the Twenty-first Century

Alexander Garvin

At the beginning of *The Death and Life of Great American Cities,* Jane Jacobs writes: "Cities are an immense laboratory of trial and error, failure and success, in city building and city design. This is the laboratory in which city planning should have been learning and forming and testing theories. Instead the practitioners and teachers of this discipline (if such it can be called) have ignored the study of success and failure in real life, have been incurious about the reasons for unexpected success, and are guided instead by principles . . . and imaginary dream cities—from anything but cities themselves."[1] All but one of the authors of the essays in this book have done what Jacobs recommended: they have gone out to study real projects in real cities and report back on the current state of planning in the United States. From what they have told us, we know the "imaginary dream cities" Jacobs inveighed against no longer provide the basis for city building and city design.

Governments no longer emphasize the large-scale City Beautiful projects that Jacobs derided, as "one heavy monument after another was . . . sorted out from the rest of the city, and assembled into the grandest effect thought possible."[2] Nor do they still propose the Utopian landscape of towers in the park that she observed were "so orderly, so visible, so easy to understand . . . but as to how the city works" told "nothing but lies."[3]

The third imaginary dream city she opposed consisted of low-to-medium density residences grouped around common open space. She thought they were "powerful and city-destroying" places. In fact, this suburban dream and its single-family home on an eighth-of-an-acre counterpart turned out to be the very popular reality that Peter Calthorpe in his essay "From New Regionalism to the Urban Network" now proposes to replace with "transit-oriented" developments at comparable densities.

Jacobs proposed that we reproduce the sort of high-density neighborhood in which she lived when her book was published in 1961: Manhattan's West Village. This was a lively, heterogeneous neighborhood that included buildings of different ages, used by many different people for different purposes at different times of the day. Her recommendation became the inspiration for urbanists around the country.

However much planning was inspired by imaginary dream cities, public action to improve cities throughout the twentieth century has consisted of projects, plans, and processes that grew out of the requirements of implementation rather than images of an ideal future. The three most effective urban planners of the twentieth century were virtuosos in their use. Robert Moses concentrated on projects. Daniel Burnham conceived the country's first comprehensive plans. Edmund Bacon used the very process of planning to transform Philadelphia.

Moses probably built more projects than any other public official at any time, anywhere. In New York City alone he created seven big bridges (spanning 28 miles), two major tunnels (3 miles), thirteen parkways (108 miles), eighteen highways (101 miles), and 658 playgrounds, and he added 17 miles of public beach to the single mile of public beach and 20,200 acres of parks to the 14,800 acres that existed when he became NYC Parks Commissioner in 1934. As chairman of the Mayor's Committee on Slum Clearance, between 1948 and 1960, when he retired from city government, he proposed fifty-nine urban renewal projects of which only twenty-three (involving 39,236 new apartments) were completed, often in greatly altered form.

The "62 major economic development initiatives launched since Mayor Bloomberg took office," like the hundreds built by Moses, will change New York forever.[4] However, it is misleading to imply, as Susan Fainstein does in "The Return of Urban Renewal," that lots of projects constitute "comprehensive planning." Nevertheless, as she explains, Bloomberg's projects, like those of Moses, demand "big, long-term visions." The difference between the projects advanced by Moses and those proposed by Bloomberg's deputy mayor, Daniel Doctoroff, lies in the degree of disruption that these projects will cause. The twenty-three urban renewal projects that Moses initiated involved the relocation of somewhere between the 21,375 families identified by the city's housing agencies and the 22,529 families enumerated on those sites in the 1950 census. Although this is a far cry from the "at least half a million" Fainstein alleges were displaced by Moses's urban renewal and highway building programs, his projects did destroy entire neighborhoods. More important, they made it impossible for the Bloomberg administration or any public agency in the State of New York to conceive of projects involving substantial relocation. That is why the Hudson Yards Project (popularly thought of as consisting only of a new Jets Stadium) covers rail yards where nobody lives or does business. (It is the overall plan for the surrounding area that may displace 139 residents.) That is also why none of the current sixty-two major economic development projects involves serious neighborhood dislocation or residential relocation.

Most planning today, as during the twentieth century, still takes place on a project-by-project basis, even extraordinarily expensive, time-consuming projects like Boston's Central Artery Project, so ably described by Hubert Murray in "Paved with Good Intentions." The so-called Big Dig was made possible by billions of dollars in federal subsidies. Fortunately, it is not at all like the cataclysmic redevelopment schemes that the federal government once subsidized. In Boston, as in New York and the rest of the country, projects that cause massive dislocation are no longer politically feasible.

A second form of twentieth-century planning—comprehensive city strategies—still takes place but much less prominently than during the decades that followed the publication of Daniel Burnham and Edward Bennett's 1909 *Plan of Chicago*. Cities as diverse as Baton Rouge and Washington, DC, have issued major city plans. Jonathan Barnett presents the fascinating story of "Omaha by Design—All of It," which, like Burnham and Bennett's classic work, deals with an entire city. The Wallace Roberts and Todd plan he describes is only the last in a series of plans that Omaha issued in 1946, 1957, 1966, 1973, and 1997. Some components of these plans were implemented, others were not. The same will be true of this latest plan. Nor is Omaha unique in its planning history. California, Florida, and other states require municipalities to create and update comprehensive plans. While some states require zoning and private development to be consistent with the plan, no state requires that a comprehensive plan be implemented. What may point in a new direction for the twenty-first century is the approach taken in this last, 2004 plan, described by Barnett. The plan uses topography to create a framework for designing parks and open space, public buildings, and neighborhood plans. This return to the sort of physical planning common between the First and Second World Wars represents an approach to city making that may well set a standard for the future.

The third twentieth-century city planning mechanism emphasizes process rather than projects or plans. In 1947 in Philadelphia, Edmund Bacon and a group of reformers organized the exhibition *A Better Philadelphia.* At that exhibition, attended by 385,000 people during the two months it was open, Bacon and his colleagues set forth a series of proposals that kept changing over the next three decades in response to public demands and financial reality until the proposals were ready for implementation and emerged on the landscape. This is the approach I took in planning the redevelopment of Lower Manhattan after the September 11th attack and in the planning for New York City's bid for the 2012 Olympic Games.

As John Kaliski demonstrates in "Democracy Takes Command," the public now demands a role in the planning process. When Los Angeles created a network of advisory neighborhood councils in its 1999 charter revision, it was simply institutionalizing that process, something that for many years had been part of the city charters of New York City, Atlanta, and many other cities.

Urban planning, whether based on projects, plans, or process, works only when the results are feasible simultaneously in physical, functional, financial, and political ways. Having merely one or two of these feasibilities just won't work. This is made clear in Richard Plunz and Michael Sheridan's "Deadlock Plus 50" and Peter Calthorpe's "From New Regionalism to the Urban Network."

Plunz and Sheridan tell the story of New York City's Housing Authority (NYCHA). It is an important story because the agency owns and operates more than 180,000 apartments in public housing projects that provide homes for a population greater than that of Boston, Denver, or Seattle. NYCHA was the first public housing agency in the country, established by Mayor Fiorello La Guardia in 1934. Its success is due to a dedicated staff that prides itself on physically, functionally, financially, and politically feasible projects that they manage with great effectiveness.

As Plunz and Sheridan point out, unlike people in many cities, nobody in New York would dream of tearing down public housing. Even though most architecture critics consider NYCHA projects ugly, inhumane, and depersonalizing, 240,000 families are on the agency's list waiting to get in. Adventurous design would not have satisfied federal design, construction, and financial specifications. During the 1930s, 1940s, and 1950s, when the federal government appropriated huge sums for low-income housing, the agency built and built and built. As Plunz and Sheridan explain, this building hit an impasse. Recent federal programs for low-income housing, such as Section 8 and Low Income Housing Tax Credits (Section 42), are not intended as tools for government agencies. Moreover, NYCHA tenants would never accept the demolition of low-cost apartments that is inherent in the only recent program that applied to public housing, the HOPE VI Program. Thus, NYCHA is now a relic of mid-twentieth-century politics and government financing that is no longer available and thus not a model for twenty-first-century planning.

Peter Calthorpe has been advocating suburban transit-oriented development for almost two decades. His ideas are logically indisputable. They could be and were implemented during the nineteenth and early twentieth centuries when local governments invested heavily in mass transit. With exceptions in a small number of wealthy communities, however, Calthorpe's approach is unlikely to have widespread appeal during the twenty-first century. It may be an attractive physical proposition, but it is precisely the sort of imaginary dream city that Jane Jacobs decried. And it is a dream, lacking functional, financial, or political feasibility. Here is why:

Transit-oriented development at the high densities permitted around subway stations in Chicago, New York, or even Bethesda, Maryland, generate adequate real estate taxes to justify their capital cost. User charges cover a substantial portion of their operating costs; government subsidies cover the rest. User charges, however, cannot cover anywhere near the same proportion of transit operating costs at the low densities typical of most suburban communities or even at the augmented suburban densities Calthorpe proposes. Some wealthier communities may be willing to pay the capital cost of installing such systems, but very few are willing to pay for their huge operating losses. More important, the substantial government subsidies needed to cover operating losses are not likely to be granted by legislative bodies. Still more important, very few suburban homeowners are likely to approve the zoning changes that would make possible construction of the apartment buildings that would have to replace existing one-family houses.

Where We Are Now

The context for planning has changed significantly since *The Death and Life of Great American Cities* first appeared. The essays in this book challenge readers to think long and hard about what works and what doesn't. Equally important, they should force them to decide what is and what is not in the public interest.

Communities no longer tolerate projects, plans, or even a planning process that does not include widespread public participation. One reason is that preservationists have obtained legislation preventing wholesale destruction of our cultural heritage. Another is that most states now require an analysis of every possible environmental impact prior to the construction of major projects. And everywhere government agencies and developers face opposition from people who do not want a proposed project in their backyard or, often, anywhere.

The role of government itself has changed. Local spending is devoted largely to providing costly services that received minor budget allocations or none at all during the earlier part of the twentieth century. A substantial proportion of federal spending is now devoted primarily to entitlements, debt service, and the military. Furthermore, unlike the 1950s and 1960s, when federal highway and urban renewal funds required and paid for comprehensive planning, today planning is usually the first item to be cut from increasingly tight government budgets.

Consequently, in many places real estate developers have taken up the planning function. Projects like Cityplace, a "lifestyle" shopping center in West Palm Beach; Central Station, a large-scale residential development just south of the loop in Chicago; and Lindbergh Center, a mixed-use, transit-oriented complex built above one of Atlanta's subway stations, were conceived as individual projects in response to market demand rather than comprehensive planning.

Nonprofit developers are becoming important players in the planning game. One of the first was Phipps Houses, a nonprofit organization founded in 1905. A century later, it has an annual operating budget of $55 million, has developed more than six thousand affordable apartments, and manages nearly fourteen thousand apartments. Bridge, another nonprofit organization, was established in 1983 to alleviate the shortage of affordable housing in the San Francisco Bay area. As of 2005 it had developed more than eleven thousand units. Perhaps the most important of the housing-based nonprofits is New York's Community Preservation Corporation. Since its establishment in 1974 to "provide mortgage, construction, and other lending for the housing needs and the ancillary commercial activities that are necessary for achieving sustainable communities,"[5] it has provided over $4.1 billion of public and private funds that paid for the construction and rehabilitation of more than 110,000 housing units. Nonprofit organizations like these are beginning to play roles once reserved for government officials like Robert Moses and government agencies such as NYCHA.

The role of the nonprofits extends far beyond housing. In discussing the impact of Deputy Mayor Doctoroff in "The Return of Urban Renewal," Susan Fainstein is right to credit Mayor Bloomberg with a major shift in government policy. It is the harbinger of a better direction for twenty-first-century planning. However, she overlooks the fact that many of Mayor Bloomberg's initiatives began life as plans that I conceived for NYC2012, the nonprofit organization Doctoroff founded to bring the Olympic Games to New York in 2012. These plans included building a stadium (usable for the Olympics) over the Hudson Yards, extending number seven subway service to Eleventh Avenue, expanding the Jacobs Javits Convention Center, creating a new park on the East River waterfront in Williamsburg, Brooklyn, and making a 4,500-apartment Olympic Village part of the Queens West Development Project.

Nonprofit organizations with a national base, like the Trust for Public Land, the National Trust for Historic Preservation, and Habitat for Humanity, are also generating planning initiatives. In 2004, for example, the Georgia Office of the Trust for Public Land commissioned my firm to devise a way to increase public green space acreage in Atlanta. We created a plan for the 2,544-acre Beltline Emerald Necklace, a twenty-three-mile-long combination of trails and transit encircling downtown Atlanta, including four expanded parks, four new parks, and five mixed-use, park-centered developments. Mayor

Shirley Franklin announced her support for the project in early 2005, appointed Ray Weeks, an experienced local developer, to spearhead its development, and by the time this essay is printed will have submitted legislation to create a tax allocation district that will generate more than $1.8 billion to pay for it.

Planning for the Twenty-first Century

Given the changing combination of players in the planning game and as these essays illustrate, we need to establish a clear and effective planning role for government. Several of the essays in this book lay out the central elements of that role. They include:

1. establishing, growing, and maintaining an emphasis on the public realm as a framework for private and nonprofit development;
2. establishing and continually updating intelligent, flexible guidelines for private, nonprofit, and public development;
3. establishing and continually updating incentives for private and nonprofit development; and
4. avoiding planning for single-function development.

Some localities may adopt a public realm framework of scenic drives along ridge lines, creek valleys, and tree-lined streets such as the one Jonathan Barnett describes in "Omaha by Design—All of It." Others may choose to increase the amount of public parkland and enhance the street grid by creating pedestrian/bicycle arteries, extending the street grid to the water's edge, and reducing the presence of automobile traffic and parking in ways similar to those presented in Leonie Sandercock's "An Anatomy of Civic Ambition in Vancouver." These cities have set a fine direction for twenty-first-century planning.

Some cities are taking new approaches to regulating development. Vancouver, as Sandercock explains, has adopted a more open participatory process for regulating design and construction. Its Urban Design Advisory Panel—consisting of two representatives each from the real estate industry, the design professions, and the general public—has adopted specifications that encourage construction particularly appropriate to Vancouver's spectacular waterfront site. That city's townhouse podium with towers above may not be appropriate to many other cities. But adjusting zoning regulations to local conditions is surely the right approach for twenty-first-century planning.

Many cities have established incentives to obtain specific forms of development. New York City, for example, has a long history of using incentives. It adopted the country's first program of tax exemption for new housing construction in 1920 and the first tax exemption and abatement for housing rehabilitation in 1955. There is much to learn from these and other NYC incentive programs. But as Lynn Becker points out in "Can Planning Be a Means to Better Architecture?" it is Chicago that is now leading the way. Its 2004 zoning ordinance provides incentives for placing parking below grade and for wrapping above-grade parking with occupiable space.

This book also highlights planning that doesn't work. In virtually every case, such planning is the result of a single entity pursuing single-function projects. Hubert Murray presents the most dramatic of these, the Massachusetts Highway Department's Central Artery/Third Harbor Tunnel, in "Paved with Good Intentions." As he explains, this project originated as a transportation proposal in 1972. It continues to be a transportation project, despite substantial public review, open space proposals, and seaport development. As Matthew J. Kiefer points out in "Public Planning and Private Initiative," planning the South Boston waterfront involved federal, state, and city agencies but relied as much on requirements imposed by government bodies as it did on $14.5 billion from Washington. Effective planning cannot take place if it is entirely a matter of single-function programmatic mandates. Atlanta's Beltline Emerald Necklace offers a far better model for twenty-first-century planning by combining transit with 2,014 acres of new and expanded parkland and 530 acres for mixed-use, public/private development.

While it is important to avoid single-function planning, it is even more important *not* to transform the promising models presented in this book into imaginary dream cities, such as those Jacobs warned against nearly half a century ago. Cities and neighborhoods are different from one another. Adopting a single model to be applied globally is a recipe for failure.

Instead, we should learn from planning that works. Like Omaha, we should be adjusting our public realm to the capabilities of local topography. Like Chicago, we should be recognizing the importance of history. Frank Gehry's band shell in the city's new Millennium Park is simply the latest addition to Daniel Burnham's 1896 proposed transformation of a lakeshore brownfield into what has become Grant Park. Most important, as Jerold Kayden's "Is Eminent Domain for

Economic Development Constitutional?" demonstrates, public intervention into the private market can go too far, stimulating an angry backlash from abused property owners. Effective planning must demonstrate beyond any reasonable doubt that whatever public action is taken (and the private market reaction it generates) will be in the public interest physically, functionally, financially, politically, and, as Kayden explains, aesthetically and spiritually as well. The essays in this book provide valuable insights into planning that does and doesn't achieve these goals.

Notes

1. Jane Jacobs, *The Death and Life of Great American Cities* (New York: Random House, 1961), 6.
2. Ibid., 24–25.
3. Ibid., 23.
4. Deputy Mayor Doctoroff's words, quoted in Susan Fainstein's essay in this volume.
5. Community Preservation Corporation, "Statement of Mission," www.communityp.com/index.php?sec=main&page=mission.

1

The Return of Urban Renewal: Dan Doctoroff's Grand Plans for New York City

Susan S. Fainstein

For many years, New York City refrained from any semblance of comprehensive planning. Even the four megaprojects of the 1980s and 1990s—Battery Park City, the Javits Convention Center, and Times Square redevelopment, all in Manhattan, and MetroTech in central Brooklyn—represented isolated endeavors rather than parts of an overriding vision. Suddenly, however, the current mayor, Michael R. Bloomberg, and his deputy mayor for economic development, Daniel L. Doctoroff, have ambitions for remaking much of the city on a scale comparable to the remaking overseen by Robert Moses in the 1940s and 1950s. Indeed, the map showing "selected planning and economic development initiatives" within a recent city publication reminds one of the similar map displaying Robert Moses's undertakings shown on the inside cover of Robert Caro's biography of the city's last powerful development czar.[1] Deputy Mayor Doctoroff, who currently masterminds the city's energetic program, consciously evokes the grandeur of Daniel Burnham's famous injunction to make no small plans.[2] He presents the "62 major economic development initiatives launched since Mayor Bloomberg took office" as based on a "supreme confidence in the future of New York . . . that demands big, long-term visions. That's why we sometimes speak in billions, not millions . . . and why our horizon stretches for decades, not months."[3]

This expansive view of the planning function and the role of government in directing it hearkens back to the early years of urban renewal in the United States. It constitutes a rejection of the timidity that followed the downfall of the federal urban renewal program.[4] The question for planners and designers is whether to applaud this new vigor or to see in it all the pitfalls that ultimately led to the demise of the old urban renewal program, ultimately excoriated by neighborhood residents, progressive critics, business interests, and the U.S. Congress, albeit for different reasons.

Urban Renewal in New York

New York City was a pioneer in the creation of megaprojects for urban transformation. Even before the passage of the 1949 Housing Act setting up the federal Title I program for urban renewal, New York implemented two large redevelopment schemes resulting in large-scale displacement of residents and businesses: Stuyvesant Town and the United Nations complex. Between 1945 and 1960, under Robert Moses's leadership, urban renewal and highway building programs displaced at least half a million New Yorkers from their homes, built a roughly similar number of new housing units, created Lincoln Center for the Performing Arts, and produced the arterial system that crisscrosses the city and connects it to its hinterland.[5]

After 1960, public opinion, reacting to the destruction of urban fabric and community life caused by Moses's programs, turned against massive redevelopment schemes involving demolition. The city then entered a second phase in which, for the most part, urban renewal no longer involved extensive clearance but did still aim at widespread change. Zoning incentives and public money stimulated continued large-scale commercial construction in Manhattan, and under the state's Mitchell-Lama program for moderate-income housing, thousands of new housing units went up. With the exception of the World Trade Center development, built on land formerly occupied by a thriving group of small businesses, these later activities involved conscious efforts at neighborhood preservation. Two projects, Roosevelt Island and Co-Op City—huge moderate- and middle-income housing developments—were built on vacant land. At the same time, under the aegis of the War on Poverty and the Model Cities program, increasing sums of money were spent in efforts to revive neighborhoods that had been devastated by middle-class suburbanization and the withdrawal of investment.[6] Construction projects in these areas mostly involved rehab or building on empty lots. In line with reforms mandated in the amended federal urban renewal law, citizens of affected areas participated in the planning of redevelopment efforts and were entitled to adequate relocation assistance.

A series of events in the 1970s marked the end of the far-reaching programs that had characterized the postwar period. Although the City Planning Commission had proposed a master plan in 1969, enthusiasm for planning and funding for its implementation died during the ensuing decade. New York State financing of affordable housing ended; President Nixon imposed a moratorium on federal housing subsidies; the 1974 Housing and Community Development Act terminated the Urban Renewal, Public Housing, and Model Cities programs, substituting the Community Development Block Grant (CDBG) and Section 8. The former did not provide sufficient funds to replicate the large projects funded by Title I, and the latter mainly involved subsidies to consumers of housing rather than for its construction. New York's 1975 fiscal crisis resulted in the freezing of the city's own capital budget. In the following twenty-five years, after plans for Westway, a gigantic highway and real-estate development on Manhattan's West Side, were scuttled in 1989, many saw in that defeat a precedent indicating that nobody could ever build anything of major proportions in New York again.

Why a Revival Now?

The efforts under way now are being carried out in the name of economic development rather than of the elimination of blight and slum clearance. In their physical manifestations, which in many cases incorporate mixed-use developments and retention of the street grid, they represent an absorption of Jane Jacobs's invective against the dullness created by city planning under urban renewal. But even though they are not Modernist in their physical forms, they are in their functional aims.[7] As in the first stage of urban renewal, they represent the imprint of a master builder rather than community-based planning. Participation by citizens is restricted to their testimony at public hearings, listening to presentations by the plans' progenitors, and the provision of advice by the community board for the affected area.[8] Beyond these minimal requirements under the Uniform Land Use Review Procedure (ULURP),[9] no legislation imposes community input. One reason for the waning popularity of the federal urban renewal program among business leaders was that as citizen participation requirements got more stringent, it became increasingly difficult to mold plans to business desires. Now, use of New York State's Empire State Development Corporation as the implementing body for projects exempts them from the ULURP process, as would not be the case if a city agency were the sponsor. Financing that does not draw from the city's capital budget frees them from city council oversight.

In the aggregate, the various projects represent a comprehensive effort to make use of the waterfront for new property development and recreation, to revive decayed commercial districts, to build and renovate housing throughout the city, to develop infrastructure, and to connect physical changes with economic opportunity. These projects consist of new and rehab construction, zoning changes, business and tourism promotion, and workforce development. Some of them—especially better access to the waterfront, improvements for parks and recreation, and additions to the housing stock—enjoy wide support. But projects aimed at major changes of use have attracted considerable opposition and appear to replicate many of the qualities that turned people against urban renewal. These include insensitivity to community desires, overly optimistic predictions concerning ultimate use, and the favoring of large over small business interests. Further, without the backing provided by federal funds, they incorporate highly risky financial commitments. Closer examination of some of the proposals points to, on the one hand, their ambitiousness and alleged benefits, and, on the other, their pitfalls.

Currently Proposed Projects

Manhattan's West Side

By far the largest in scope and most controversial of the mayor's sixty-two initiatives is the plan for the Far West Side of Manhattan. The focal point of conflict is the proposed 75,000-seat football stadium, to be built on a deck over the Penn Central railroad yards at a cost estimated at $1.4 billion.[10] While the stadium has attracted the most attention, the plan calls for major changes in a sixty-block area west

Rendering, opening ceremonies, Olympic Stadium, 2012 Olympic bid, Manhattan, New York. Photograph copyright NYC2012, inc.

of Eighth Avenue between Twenty-eighth and Forty-second Streets. Currently a mix of old and new businesses in small-scale structures, the area would be transformed into an extension of the midtown central business district. The city's draft environmental review estimates that at least 225 businesses, 4,269 employees, and 139 residents in ten buildings would be directly displaced as a result of demolitions. In their place would be a new boulevard extending from Thirty-fourth Street to Forty-second Street between Tenth and Eleventh Avenues and a series of high-rise office buildings, hotels, and residential structures.

Attracting commercial developers to the area would require an extension of the number seven subway line.

The plan raises a host of issues, many of them arising out of differing forecasts of its impact. The city assumes that the sports and convention facility will generate economic development in its surrounding environment, even though experience in other cities has shown otherwise.[11] The West Side scheme calls for construction of millions of square feet of new office space, even while other plans call for ten million square feet to be built in downtown Manhattan and the construction of large office centers in Brooklyn and Queens. Given the present level of vacancies, it seems very unlikely that, even with optimistic estimates of growth in office jobs, any additional space would be needed before 2009, and more conservative forecasts indicate it would take until 2015 before any new office construction beyond that already on the drawing board would be needed.[12] Moreover, office take-up projections are based on extrapolations from past experience, but the past may no longer be a useful guide. New technology that allows office workers to conduct their business almost anywhere makes predictions regarding the office needs of the future unreliable.

Union laborers rally for development plan to build stadium on Manhattan's West Side for the N.Y. Jets and to expand the Jacob K. Javits Convention Center, Madison Square Garden, New York, September 2004. Photograph by Mary Altaffer; courtesy of the Associated Press.

The West Side plan resembles early urban renewal planning in its specification of changed uses, its scope, its reliance on eminent domain of occupied property for land acquisition, and its optimism that private developers will come along to fulfill the plan's goals. It puts the city itself at much greater financial risk than did the earlier model, however. Whereas urban renewal authorities could rely on federal funds to insulate themselves from the speculative aspects of their projects, current city proposals rely on locally supplied funding. The city's plans propose that a corporation be established that would issue bonds to pay for infrastructure including the subway extension and the platform and deck of the stadium. Theoretically these bonds would be paid off with tax revenues generated by the new development. A letter from the city's controller, however, warns that it is "a project that could yield little return to City taxpayers and may in fact cost them billions of dollars . . . if revenues from the project do not materialize."[13]

In a further resemblance to the first period of urban renewal, the stadium project avoids legislative oversight. Doctoroff, on the one hand, frankly admits that no approval by a democratically elected body will occur.[14] On the other, when asked by an interviewer whether he should be compared to Robert Moses, he disclaims the resemblance, contending that "There's clearly an opportunity to transform the physical landscape now, but . . . it has to be the result of substantial community input, if not consensus."[15] Of course, Doctoroff does serve at the pleasure of the mayor, who is an elected official and must face the voters in 2005. Moses, in contrast, headed an independent authority and could be unseated only with great difficulty.

The Bronx Terminal Market

The Bronx Terminal Market houses twenty-three wholesale food merchants in deteriorated buildings just south of Yankee Stadium.[16] The city, which already owns the market site, has agreed with the Related Companies, a development firm that recently took over the lease for the site, to move the merchants to another, as yet undisclosed location. The existing buildings would be demolished to make way for a retail shopping mall, a big-box store, and a hotel. The development plan will be subject to the normal ULURP process and already has the endorsement of the Bronx borough president.[17]

Constructed in the 1920s, the market was originally located to take advantage of access to waterborne transportation on the Harlem River. Subsequently it benefited from the construction of I-95 and the Major Deegan Expressway, which provided convenient access for large trucks. Although the market structures are not fully occupied and are in a serious state of disrepair, the market continues to serve a large number of both wholesale and retail customers and to employ approximately 750 people, about half of whom live in the Bronx. It provides stable employment for people with relatively low levels of education, many of them immigrants lacking language skills. Its competitive advantage rests on the clustering of similar businesses selling primarily to ethnic food stores; although competitors, the businesses assist each other and cooperate in management of the facility. The market allows patrons the convenience of one-stop shopping and offers proximity to the bridges to Manhattan and to public transit.

As in the demolition of downtown's Radio Row to allow for construction of the World Trade Center, the razing of the Bronx Terminal Market to accommodate a "higher and better use" would enhance city revenues at the cost of destroying a viable business cluster. The change in use would result in a transformation of the employment structure of the area: whereas almost all the present workers are male and many are unionized, the clerks in the new retail stores would be predominantly low-paid women. If the relocation of the merchants does not cause them to lose their customer base, this would constitute a net gain for Bronx residents. The merchants fear, however, that they will be moved to a less convenient location and, as a result, be forced out of business, as has happened to other New York food wholesalers. Hence evaluation of the likely outcomes of the project depends on the relocation plan. But while the intention of evicting the merchants has been made public, their ultimate location remains unknown.

Downtown Brooklyn

In central Brooklyn, another proposal for building a sports facility over railroad yards has emerged. Developer Bruce Ratner, who has been the main sponsor of projects in downtown Brooklyn, purchased the New Jersey Nets basketball team with the intention of bringing them to Brooklyn. The $2.5-billion, 7.7-million-square-foot mixed-use project, with the Nets arena as its centerpiece, would be built on eleven acres of MTA-owned land and about eleven acres of privately owned property. Using the instrument of the state's Empire State Development Corporation, which has the power to override local zoning in the city, the government would condemn property in the case of the owner's refusal to sell. The size of the project, the use of eminent domain, and the top-down nature of its formulation all hearken back to the early days of urban renewal. The difference, as stated by one commentator, is that "the private market has already brought this area back. There's one thing different from the old urban renewal: there's not even a pretense of blight to justify condemnation subsidies."[18]

The area of Brooklyn slated for renewal is undergoing substantial gentrification. Interestingly, unlike the proponents of the West Side stadium, the developer is not justifying his proposal in terms of benefits that would flow directly from the basketball arena. Rather, the stadium is viewed as a kind of loss leader—it is the associated housing, office, and retail developments that are anticipated to be the source of developers' profit and city revenues.[19] Supporters of the development point to its substantial component of new housing for low- and moderate-income occupants. As in the case of the Bronx Terminal Market and to

Frank Gehry, model for Brooklyn Arena and "Urban Room." Courtesy of www.bball.net.

a lesser extent of the Far West Side, this Brooklyn project is a move by government to invest public funds and utilize condemnation powers to make property yield a higher rate of return.

The New Urban Renewal

The justification in all three cases primarily stems from their economic contribution rather than their physical improvements. Taxpayers' money would be put at risk in the expectation of projected revenues and employment. The three sites have been selected on the basis of proximity to either central Manhattan (for the West Side Yards and downtown Brooklyn) or highway access (for the Bronx Terminal Market). The city has excluded affected residents and businesses from participating in planning, limiting their participation to reacting to already formulated plans and gaining at best minor concessions. The Bronx and Brooklyn schemes have the endorsements of the respective borough presidents, although the Manhattan borough president opposes the West Side stadium. The plans are subject to the political process in that their financing is from the city and state, and their progenitors are locally elected public officials. No alternative plans have been presented for comparison, however, and each has been presented as the only possibility. In the Brooklyn and Bronx projects, a developer has been preselected for the sites without solicitation of competitive bids or the opportunity for anyone to suggest other development strategies.

Advocates for the projects cite NIMBYism as the basis for objections. Opponents generally argue that changes in zoning would be sufficient to attract private development without the use of eminent domain and would result in construction that responded to market forces. Many feel that the demand for office space will not in the foreseeable future take up the amount of space being projected by the numerous office-based proposals outlined in the city's economic development initiatives.

For planners who do not believe that the market always produces choices best for the city, seeing the city once again engaged in planning that makes explicit the changes to come is welcome. Thus, in one respect, the current thrust toward comprehensiveness and public investment is a step forward in making visible and contested a process that otherwise remains hidden. But the methods by which the plans are developed, the emphasis on sports complexes, the encumbrances on the city's and state's fiscal integrity, and the sheer magnitude and density of the proposed projects can only cause serious misgivings.

In the first phase of the federal urban renewal program, opponents of projects that would destroy communities and small business were similarly excoriated for being unconcerned with the public interest.[20] It was only later, when it became evident that benefits did not always trickle down, communities were destroyed, cleared land lay vacant for decades awaiting a developer, and "marginal" businesses that frequently laid the groundwork for the next wave of innovation were uprooted, that the dangers of "great plans" became fully appreciated. By now many of these lessons have been forgotten as a new generation of architects and planners has come along seeking to imprint their visions on New York's landscape. The pendulum has swung to the other side rather than resting at a point where comprehensive planning can occur within a context of humility, flexibility, and democratic participation.

Notes

1. City of New York, Michael R. Bloomberg, Mayor, "Bloomberg Administration: Major Economic Development Initiatives," n.d. (distributed in 2004); Robert Caro, *The Power Broker* (New York: Knopf, 1974).

2. The combination of Mayor Michael Bloomberg and Doctoroff is reminiscent of the earlier one of Mayor Robert Lee of New Haven and his development administrator, Ed Logue, in its mustering of political clout behind a plan to transform a city.

3. Speech at Crain's Breakfast Forum, New York Hilton, September 29, 2004.

4. Altshuler and Luberoff, in their recent study of megaprojects, comment that such schemes have become exceptional and that most new development is modest in scale and does not involve demolition. See Alan A. Altshuler and David Luberoff, *Mega-Projects: The Changing Politics of Urban Public Investment* (Washington, DC: Brookings Institution, 2003).

5. Norman I. Fainstein and Susan S. Fainstein, "Governing Regimes and the Political Economy of Development in New York City, 1946–1984," in *Power, Culture, and Place: Essays on New York City,* ed. John Hull Mollenkopf (New York: Russell Sage Foundation, 1988), 164–71.

6. Ibid., 171–81.

7. See James C. Scott, *Seeing Like a State* (New Haven: Yale University Press, 1998).

8. New York's community boards are appointed by the city council members for their district and by the borough president. They exercise advisory power over land use and capital budget matters.

9. The Uniform Land Use Review Process requires a series of approvals and includes scrutiny by the district's community board.

10. It seems likely that the actual costs would exceed the estimated $1.4 billion. See Bent Flyvbjerg, Nils Bruzelius, and Werner Rothengatter, *Megaprojects and Risk* (Cambridge, UK: Cambridge University Press, 2003).

11. Ziona Austrian and Mark S. Rosentraub, "Urban Tourism and Financing Professional Sports Facilities," in *Financing Economic Development,* ed. Sammis B. White, Richard D. Bingham, and Edward W. Hill (Armonk, NY: M. E. Sharpe, 2003), 211–32; Charles Euchner, "Tourism and Sports: The Serious Competition for Play," in *The Tourist City,* ed. Dennis R. Judd and Susan S. Fainstein (New Haven, CT: Yale University Press, 1999), 215–32.

12. The Regional Plan Association reluctantly decided to oppose the plans for the stadium; Regional Plan Association, "Fulfilling the Promise of Manhattan's Far West Side," Position Paper, July 2004, 13.

13. Letter from William C. Thompson Jr. to Mayor Michael Bloomberg, October 20, 2004, http://www.comptroller.nyc.gov/bureaus/opm/pdf_letters/oct-20-04_letter-bloomberg-westside.pdf.

14. Response to question at Crain's Breakfast Forum. The letter from the controller asserts: "You chose not to include this project in the capital budget, avoiding City Council approval. In doing so, you removed the public's only opportunity for meaningful and serious review of the merits of your plan against other priorities."

15. Quoted in Craig Horowitz, "Stadium of Dreams," *New York,* June 21, 2004, 22.

16. The Bronx Terminal Market should be distinguished from the much larger and more modern Hunt's Point Market to the north.

17. New York City Economic Development Corporation, News Release, April 29, 2004.

18. Julia Vitullo-Martin, "Thinking about Ratner's Urban Renewal," *Monthly Newsletter of the Manhattan Institute's Center for Rethinking Development,* May 2004, 1. Opposition to the project by the Manhattan Institute represents a conservative, pro-market viewpoint. But it supports the position of neighborhood opponents, who do not object to government intervention on ideological grounds but rather to the failure of the city to consult neighborhood residents and to its scale.

19. Andrew Zimbalist, "Estimated Fiscal Impact of the Atlantic Yards Project on the New York City and New York State Treasuries," May 1, 2004, http://www.fieldofschemes.com/documents/zimbalist.doc. Zimbalist estimates present value of all public sector costs at $699 million, providing a net positive fiscal impact with a present value of $812.7 million. See also Johannah Rod-

ger, "The Price of Ratner's Hoopla: Brooklyn Stadium Would Be a Money Loser for NYC," *Brooklyn Rail,* June 2004, http://www.brooklynrail.org/local/june04/ratnershoopla.html; Jung King and Gustave Peebles, "Estimated Fiscal Impact of Forest City Ratner's Brooklyn Arena and 17 High Rise Development on NYC and NYS Treasuries," June 21, 2004, http://www.developdontdestroy.org/public/EconReport.pdf.

20. See Langley Keyes, *The Rehabilitation Planning Game* (Cambridge, MA: MIT Press, 1969).

2

Deadlock Plus 50: On Public Housing in New York

Richard Plunz and Michael Sheridan

The New York City Housing Authority (NYCHA) is by far the city's largest landlord, presiding over 180,000 apartments with at least 600,000 tenants; its 1997 budget was $1.7 billion. NYCHA occupies a central position within the socioeconomic framework of the city; thus a grim outlook for public housing has dire implications for the entire city. The fate of New York's public housing remains tenuous, due partly to shifting federal policy and partly to shifting demographics. Today, fifty years after the Federal Housing Act of 1949, which set the standards for government housing, public housing in New York faces an uncertain future in which social and physical changes appear inevitable. Given the steady deterioration of low-income housing in New York over the past two decades and the exorbitant cost of new construction, NYCHA is now under enormous pressure to find alternative sources of revenue. At the same time, powerful political forces seek to maintain the status quo, however troubled.

Meanwhile, national housing priorities are evolving in ways not applicable to New York. Between 1995 and 1997, federal funding for the operation of public housing was reduced from $8 billion to $6 billion, and the annual contribution from the Department of Housing and Urban Development, which accounts for 90 percent of NYCHA's budget, fell from $400 million to $285 million. In New York this reduction has made it increasingly difficult to maintain public housing. At the same time, federal policy has shifted: it is now focused on replacing high-rise projects with comparatively small-scale, low-rise development. In New York, however, this policy is proving impossible to implement. While the problems of the city's public housing have worsened—its population has changed, poverty has worsened, and social isolation has grown more pronounced—the physical environments have changed little. In many respects, today's housing dilemma recalls that of midcentury, which prompted Lewis Mumford's 1950 assessment of the early progress of the large-scale NYCHA projects: "to correct a pathological condition, [the NYCHA] employed a pathological solution."[1]

Criticism of postwar public housing crescendoed in the late 1950s, when the national architectural media became aggressively negative. By then the problems were obvious. Public housing had devolved to "low-cost" housing. Indeed, it was planned to be "housing" and nothing more: it included no traditional urbanism, not even retail, the provision of which was left to the private sector. Cost constraints made the high-rise "tower-in-the-park" the convenient model. Given various political taboos, the "park" was assumed to be the only option for site, or "landscape," development. New York was more heavily affected by high-rise construction than any other U.S. city. Already by 1957, of the 87,000 public apartments constructed in New York, approximately 45,000 (52 percent) were higher than eight stories. This critical mass established specific kinds of urban spatial typology and social management. By the 1990s, the proportion of high-rise towers was 64 percent (approximately 115,000 apartments out of 180,000).

In 1957 *Architectural Forum* published a series of articles, including Catherine Bauer's "The Dreary Deadlock of Public Housing," which was significant in many ways. A prolific author, Bauer had already written a book, *Modern Housing* (1934), that had influenced national policy and design for two decades, and an important article, "Architectural Opportunities in Public Housing," published in *Architectural Record* in 1938.[2] Appearing at the beginning and end of this formative period for public housing, these publications contain an impressive if depressing indictment. In the 1930s, Bauer's primary models were the European socialist housing experiments of the 1920s and 1930s—government-sponsored housing was not built in the United States until the Great Depression. At the time Bauer had no reason to suspect that "socialism" in America could so quickly degenerate into "pathology." Nor did she anticipate that the low-density suburban Siedlungen that she had admired in Europe (especially Germany) were not applicable models for the high-density "urban renewal" of American cities. In hindsight, Bauer's book was less a treatise on "modern" social housing than a retrospective look at long-established, genteel European practices, and by 1957 Bauer did not like what she saw in the United States. She placed blame squarely on high-rise typologies and on the "institutionalization" produced by their scale, standardization, and social and physical solutions.

In the same 1957 *Architectural Forum*, various writers suggested a number of now-familiar remedies for the problems of public housing: privatization, individual ownership, diversification of building types, localization of subsidies, community control, and subsidization of rents. But none acknowledged the uniquely dense New York context. For instance, although Bauer acknowledged that "New York is the one American city where apartment living also is most taken for granted," she was ambivalent about the implications of this fact—throughout the 1950s she advocated row-house typologies for public housing. In a 1952 article she had criticized the "nationwide crop of behemoths."[3] And although she suggested that New York might conceivably be dismissed—"they have only themselves to blame"—she admitted that elevator buildings already accounted for two-thirds of national public housing production. The tendency to shrug off the problems of housing in New York, and to see New York in a kind of opposition to the rest of the country, has changed little over the decades—and therein lies one of the important reasons for the current public housing deadlock.

The 600,000 inhabitants of NYCHA housing are by now entrenched as New York's "second city"—they comprise many of the city's residents who are classified as "very low income." For them, the escalating cost of housing is most burdensome. The median rent/income ratio for New Yorkers has risen from 19 percent in 1960 to over 30 percent in the 1990s; thus, for inhabitants of the second city, the NYCHA is an essential means of survival. Compared with other American cities, in New York demand for public housing is extremely high: 240,000 families are on the NYCHA waiting list. Strategies for de-densification that might work in other cities cannot work in New York. Public housing funds, which might be reduced in other cities due

James Mackenzie, Sidney Strauss, and Walter and Gillette, Jacob Riis Houses, Lower East Side, Manhattan, New York, 1949. Photograph courtesy of the New York City Housing Authority.

to decreasing demand, should in fact be increased in New York due to its increasing national share of families in need. Yet funds for New York have been reduced. This has led to deadlock. In this way the second city, whose existence many prefer to ignore, is reinforced through economic and social disinvestment. Unlike most of the "first city," the second city has been unable to evolve into something better.

Its situation seems permanent, far beyond the institutionalization Bauer deplored. The poor in New York have become a self-perpetuating parallel city. Many NYCHA families are now third generation. More than 15,000 NYCHA residents work for NYCHA, living in extreme economic and social isolation. This isolation is manifested in the image of blocks of red-brick high-rise projects, clearly "places apart." The reintegration of these places into the rest of the city is the heart of the challenge to improve public housing in New York.

The Impasse of the Status Quo

The past two decades have seen a widespread national reaction against high-rise public housing. In New York, however, the backlash has been muted, reflected mostly in relatively inexpensive strategies that do not displace existing apartments. Relatively little housing has been added—only 3,000 units in low-rise (three- to seven-story) buildings have been constructed since 1979—hardly enough to claim a typological change. During this same period, most of the apartments added to the NYCHA roster have been in older tenements rehabilitated through city receivership programs. Physical intervention in the housing towers has been limited—low fences added to the grounds, or more recently, panoptic electronic surveillance systems. Through all these changes, the only constants have been poverty, crime, and despair. Yet the residents, recognizing the chronic housing shortage and spurred by fear of displacement, seem determined to retain the status quo.

Recent efforts to redevelop NYCHA projects with HOPE VI funding illustrate the special complexities of New York. Since 1993, HOPE VI has granted $1.5 billion for the rehabilitation of existing developments nationwide: the goal is to replace high-rise projects with low-density, mixed-income townhouse developments based on New Urbanist ideas. Intended to reduce the hard-core poverty and grittiness of public housing, this strategy is in danger of being seen as a "one-size-fits-all" remedy for a range of unwieldy problems. It is already obvious that it cannot answer one of the particular needs of New York, which is that density in the city's public housing actually should be increased. Paradoxically, not only do residents not want increased densities, but they also fear any substantial "improvements" that might result in gentrification by higher-income families.

In New York, the first HOPE VI grants in 1993 included $500,000 for rehabilitation work at Beach 41st Street Houses—four thirteen-story slabs in southeast Queens. In 1995, $48 million in additional funds were granted for physical improvements and social services in the same development. Two years later, after the residents refused to accept the redevelopment of one hundred ground-level apartments into nonresidential uses and the relocation of families using Section 8 rent subsidies, HUD withdrew its HOPE VI money and started over again at the adjacent Edgemere and Arverne Houses, ten blocks away. In general, NYCHA has continued to pursue the economic integration of public housing projects into their communities as a means of fostering social stability and increased incomes. In 1997, NYCHA applied to HUD for a waiver from federal rent regulations at 16 of their 340 developments; NYCHA wanted to be able to accept more working families and to train and place residents in jobs in order to charge additional rent. But the application was cancelled after protests by tenant groups and their advocates, who feared that NYCHA would use the exemption to raise rents, evict families, and demolish or sell some developments.

Despite such resistance, the status quo cannot be maintained. Without a wider range of management policies and ownership options, fiscal shortages will become more severe, and physical and social conditions will deteriorate. Options for some degree of tenant participation in management or even ownership have been suggested for thirty years. Limited experimentation along these lines has successfully addressed the needs of only the higher-income NYCHA residents. For example, in 1992, NYCHA purchased thirty vacant buildings, mostly five-story walk-ups, from the city and renovated them for sale as cooperative apartments. Approximately four thousand applications were received for 730 apartments from residents of public housing and wait-listed families. That the buildings were in some of the more troubled parts of the South Bronx and Manhattan did not deter potential homeowners, who were attracted by (among other things) the prospect of being able to choose their neighbors.

The destruction of existing apartments and their replacement with fewer units are not a political option for NYCHA. The 240,000 families wait-listed for public housing and the extremely low vacancy rates mean that even limited demolition would be disastrous. Moreover, high construction costs and the scarcity of acceptable sites for replacement units make significant new construction impossible. By 1995, federal regulations required local housing authorities to locate new housing in mixed-income neighborhoods. But city-owned property is concentrated either in poor neighborhoods or in areas that are prohibitively expensive. Given this impasse, NYCHA was eventually permitted to divert the $230 million intended for new construction to the rehabilitation of plumbing, heating, and electrical systems in 22,624 existing units. This precedent points to an important reality: if little new construction is forthcoming and if public developments are to be economically integrated into their neighborhoods, then rehabilitating and transforming existing housing are the only option.

In the past, NYCHA has made limited attempts to upgrade its properties. In the early 1980s, the authority began a series of grounds security improvement projects, based on the "defensible space" theories of Oscar Newman. Unfortunately, the NYCHA work was based too literally on Newman's demonstration project at Clason Point Gardens, a fairly traditional development of two-story townhouses in the northeast Bronx. There, within an almost suburban site plan, Newman used symbolic barriers to define front yards and tall fences to enclose backyards. The authority then applied symbolic barriers and seating areas to many of its developments, regardless of site plan or building type, but this resulted in the surreal juxtaposition of three-foot-high fences and sixteen-story buildings. A 1998 NYCHA study, headed by the authors of this essay, assessed a number of "defensible space" installations and found them ineffective.

The residents' fears and management's hopes for the transformation of public housing both stem from the shaky assumption that a single formula can be applied everywhere and to the same degree. An overview of the evolution of U.S. public housing reveals that both fears and hopes are justified: in the nineteenth-century, efforts to improve the dreadful conditions of nineteenth-century Manhattan tenements and contemporary trends in political and economic rationalism led to a monolithic response not only in New York but across the country. Much public housing in New York City and the nation has been predicated on approaches and policies thought applicable everywhere. But the variety and diversity of development locations and housing residents make this impractical.

The real question for the future of public housing in New York City is: What steps are necessary to transform these dismal and dangerous environments into communities in which residents can improve their lives? What seems likely is that new strategies of management and tenant participation will be needed for NYCHA properties and residents, including expanded terms of resident management and ownership. Attracting and retaining residents who are employed and thus have some housing options may be the only way to prevent public housing from collapsing in crisis. A critical element in this struggle will be the transformation of the barren and ill-defined landscapes that surround high-rise apartment buildings—such spaces need to be well and clearly defined. And the "institutional" image of "towers in the wasteland" must be addressed through the introduction of multiple scales and typologies. Given that the federal government now sees demolition as the solution to many of the problems of public housing, it seems hardly radical to explore how high-rise developments might be rehabilitated physically and restructured socially and economically into viable components of the larger community.

Design Prospects

The redesign of public housing is an enormous challenge. Neither self-conscious avant-gardism nor image-driven "retrogradism" will serve to create the physical and social structures necessary for resident accountability and security. What is needed instead is an enlightened and pragmatic approach that accepts the high-rise as a physical and economic fact and that develops the additional program and enclosure needed for security and comfort. After decades of trying to create large-scale residential environments from scratch, it is thoroughly clear that city-making is a cumulative process. A geologic reading of the city illustrates both the deficiencies of public housing as well as the necessarily cumulative nature of its transformation. To view these developments as finished and beyond redemption is to recapitulate the idealized and unrealistic approaches to urbanism by which these developments were conceived. These "object fields" represent arrested infrastructural urbanism, awaiting layers of addition and alteration. While traditional urban fabrics have tended toward maximum built volume, uniform building height, and equally distributed mass, the further development of the towers in the park should entail a continuous fabric with more topographic variation—peaks and valleys.

The superblock makes manifest the problems of institutional scale and undifferentiated open space. Originally developed as a tool by which urban planning and redevelopment could be practiced at a large—indeed transformative—scale, the superblock was all too successful. More than any other physical feature of public housing, superblocks isolate residents from the surrounding fabric. The reintroduction of streets into superblocks would enhance security and create the foundation for renewed physical and social structure.

Lack of boundaries and of differentiated open space make superblocks threatening. The assumption of the early planners of public housing—that all exterior space should be public—created conditions that made social control impossible. In addition to the reinsertion of street networks, the definition of exterior spaces—for instance, into semiprivate courtyards between buildings, buffer zones between buildings and streets, and private yards for ground-level apartments—can give both physical and social dimension to what are now frightening and impersonal spaces.

The low percentage of built-up areas in NYCHA high-rise developments has left many with excess open land. Some of this surplus, particularly along the street frontages, could eventually become valuable commercial property. Given that public sentiment, the booming economy, and court orders have all worked to curtail discriminatory lending practices, the redevelopment of commercial activity within public projects could be hastened by the construction of suitable low-rise strips.

The sense of disconnection between high-rise buildings and their grounds was actually reinforced by the building design. The standardization of apartments had the odd result that an apartment on the first floor has no more access to outdoor space than one on the tenth floor. Much potential for rehabilitation lies within the buildings. The redesign of circulation cores, the expansion of apartments for extended families, the addition of stairwells at the lower levels—all these might be basic strategies. The creation of private yards for ground-level residents would further encourage the kind of low-rise fabric that would enhance social life within the developments.

Gates, fences, walls, and locks could serve to create barriers, physical as well as symbolic. Public circulation between street and building entry should be clearly defined, allowing residents and the police to control and watch access. Enclosing the perimeters of blocks to make yards with fences would also help to accentuate positive community: such places might be accessible only to those residents who overlook them or to residents of the entire building during certain hours. Although the idea of such differentiation among residents might seem shocking, most developments already have such differentiation: a de facto hierarchy, based on fear and criminal activity.

Research carried out over twenty years reinforces the need for integrated physical, social, and management initiatives in the transformation of public housing. Residents must be allowed, even compelled, to develop control over their environments. Central to this effort will be flexible management policies that help dispel the hostility that many residents feel toward the NYCHA. Such strategies might seem radical, but imagine how radical our contemporary reality would have seemed in 1965: third-generation tenantry, buildings controlled by criminals, the warehousing of the homeless, entire developments imploded at government expense. The unimaginable has become our history; we have come full circle to arrive again where we began: with isolated, albeit well-plumbed, ghettoes. It might be tempting to respond to such vast and complex pathologies with cynicism or hopelessness, but to ignore these challenges is tacitly to advocate further disintegration.

The degree to which current models of rehabilitation are impractical in New York underscores the need for multiple approaches to the deficiencies of public housing across the nation. To assume that a standardized program—favoring the destruction of viable buildings and the imposition of an urban monoculture—can be applied without regard for local circumstances has been a catastrophic mistake.

Diverse conditions should engender diverse responses. While apartment ownership is a viable solution for many residents, for many others it is not. While transformation of the "towers in the park" is appropriate in some cities, in many other cities it is not. The greatest danger is that simplistic, blanket "solutions" and "ideal" formulas will blind us to the greater pragmatic value of a range of solutions.

Notes

1. Lewis Mumford, "The Skyline: The Gentle Art of Overcrowding," *The New Yorker,* May 20, 1950, 81.

2. Catherine Bauer, "The Dreary Deadlock of Public Housing," *Architectural Forum,* May 1957, 140–42, 219, 221; also Catherine Bauer, "Architectural Opportunities in Public Housing," *Architectural Record,* January 1939, 65–68.

3. Catherine Bauer, "Clients for Housing: The Low-Income Tenant. Does He Want Supertenements?" *Progressive Architecture,* May 1952, 61–64.

3

Democracy Takes Command: The New Community Planning and the Challenge to Urban Design

John Kaliski

> Town meetings are to liberty what primary schools are to science; they bring it within the people's reach, they teach me how to use and how to enjoy it. . . . In America the people form a master who must be obeyed to the utmost limits of possibility.
>
> —*Alexis de Tocqueville,* Democracy in America

When Alexis de Tocqueville, author of *Democracy in America,* traveled through the United States in the 1830s, he was struck by the high level of citizen participation in local decision making. He also noted a "vast number of inconsiderable productions [buildings]" that populated the landscape of this democracy, a few monuments, and what he called the "blank" between these two extremes.[1] This could also be a description of Los Angeles today: City Hall, Moneo's cathedral, Gehry's Disney Hall, Mayne's Caltrans building, a visible suburban landscape, and in between a vast but swarming void. Exploring this void, however, reveals that democracy, at least in Los Angeles, is now designing the middle zone into a clear reflection of the needs and aspirations of the people who live there.

Three situations in Southern California illustrate the state of this type of planning: the expansion of Los Angeles International Airport (LAX), the building of a new shopping mall in Glendale, and the uproar caused by the city's clipping of overgrown front-yard hedges in Santa Monica. These demonstrate that citizen experts rather than planners or designers are firmly in charge of the evolution and design of the city. Most critically, these circumstances are typical of the state of infrastructure planning in the United States, and they challenge planners, architects, landscape architects, and, last and least, urban designers to reassess their roles with regard to the planning, design, and production of contemporary urbanism.

LAX

The expansion of Los Angeles International Airport affects all people in Southern California. Since the last round of improvements was completed for the 1984 Olympics, the city has been planning to expand LAX to accommodate ever-increasing passenger trips and cargo. Scenarios for growth, some of them quite fantastic—such as expanding runways thousands of feet west over the ocean—were at first quietly explored. In the late 1990s, Mayor Richard Riordan finally went public with a $13-billion proposal. His plan, promoted as a stimulus for the local economy, increased runway capacity and safety and proposed to replace the existing horseshoe of dispersed satellite terminals with a mega-facility. Riordan's plan was infrastructure wrought extra large, and, with the exception of the mayor's circle, hardly anybody, particularly the adjacent communities, liked it. Riordan's airport was thought to accommodate too many passenger trips and too much cargo, generate too much noise and too much traffic, and offer economic benefits at the expense of too many surrounding communities. Despite an aggressive top-down public outreach effort, the plan was close to failing.

The next mayor, James Hahn, used the events of September 11, 2001, to reframe the issues and the plan. Instead of tearing down the existing facility, his team suggested building a consolidated check-in facility near an adjacent freeway and connecting this facility to existing terminals using a people mover. The idea was to keep terrorists away from active airplane gates and terminals. By reducing the square footage that needed to be rebuilt, the price tag was lowered from $13 to $9 billion. Nevertheless, adjacent communities still perceived that the capacity for additional passenger trips and freight was unreasonably large. Many safety experts also saw the consolidated check-in facility as an even more opportune terrorist target than the existing terminals. At public meetings, the plan was still opposed by both the surrounding communities and the now mostly bankrupt airlines.

Sensing the collapse of the process and wanting to improve runway safety, Los Angeles Councilperson Cindy Miscikowski brokered a compromise: to bifurcate the Hahn plan into two phases. In the first, a consolidated rental car facility, a people mover connected to an adjacent light-rail line, and runway improvements to address safety would be completed at a cost of $3 billion. A subsequent phase would include the rest of Hahn's plan, which would require yet more studies, environmental review, and public input.

At the penultimate city council meeting, amid a gaggle of protesters, one councilperson rolled out a string fifty feet from his desk to a row of seats near the front of the council chamber. He then intoned with frustration that despite ten years and $130 million of planning and community input, decision makers were still having trouble approving a plan that in essence moves one runway fifty feet south. Here at last was clear demonstration of the scale of the enterprise in contrast to the size and duration of the public process. While the plan passed that day, the protests did not end. In fact, within weeks, the airport announced $1.5 billion of additional measures to mitigate noise and traffic problems in surrounding locales. Always seeking a better deal, the public continues to protest.

Mixed-Use Mall in Glendale

While the airport expansion impacts a region of 16.5 million people, the "Americana at Brand" mainly affects Glendale, a city of 330,000 just north of Los Angeles. The developer of this project, Rick Caruso, is best known for transforming Los Angeles's "Farmer's Market" into "The Grove," an outdoor mall linked by a neohistoric trolley to a 1930s-era market of stalls selling food and tourist trinkets. When The Grove attracted more than 3 million people a year, Caruso was courted by cities eager to realize similar success for their communities. In Glendale, Caruso promised to deliver an "American" town square defined by cinemas, restaurants, and stores with housing above, all wrapped around a new "green." To build this open-air downtown mall, Caruso also negotiated a $77-million city subsidy.

While some questioned the findings of blight required to promulgate the Americana, public opposition to the project was cemented when the owners of the Glendale Galleria, a competing mall located across the street, financed an alternative design. This design, perhaps

Rick Caruso, rendering of Americana at Brand, Glendale, California, 2004. Photograph courtesy of John Kaliski.

disingenuously (given its chief advocate), included less retail and less development intensity. A public spat between developers ensued. Sensing that the city council would support the Caruso project, the Galleria owners financed a citywide referendum: an up or down vote on the Americana. Expert designers, consensus planners, or even informed decision makers were not going to determine the future use of downtown Glendale. After an intense campaign lasting several months and costing several million dollars, Caruso won with 51 percent of the vote: the Americana at Brand was approved in an exercise of direct democracy.

Santa Monica Hedges

In Southern California even the smallest design details are now subject to the propositions and will of the voters. In Santa Monica, a city of 100,000 just west of Los Angeles, a little-known and unenforced ordinance has restricted the height of front-yard hedges for decades. Reflecting a late-nineteenth-century townscape ideal, the ordinance was meant to maintain the open sensibility of a once sleepy and somewhat seedy seaside resort. Today Santa Monica is a redoubt of wealthy homeowners who seek to shut out their urbanized surrounds.

Citing urban concerns ("People are living on top of each other"), privacy concerns ("People are always peering at us"), environmentalism ("Greenery should never be cut down"), safety concerns ("Our children can no longer play in the streets and must stay in the yard"), and property rights, many home owners grew tall hedges to wall themselves off from the city. However, not everybody in Santa Monica felt comfortable with the change to community character. Some complained that city ordinances should be enforced. When the issue was brought to city officials, the city first acknowledged and then enforced its laws; it issued citations to property owners with high hedges and eventually cut down some of the offending greenery.

City workers cutting down hedges on private property of course outraged hedge owners. Others were put off by city rationales—"The law is the law"—as well as the seeming rudeness of city council members who in public meetings initially dismissed the issue as a nuisance impacting only a few. The hedge owners organized and broadcast a critique of the city leadership and policies. A new leader emerged, Bobby Shriver, the nephew of the late Robert F. Kennedy. Shriver promised to forge a compromise that allows people to keep their hedges. He also announced that he was running for Santa Monica City Council.

Hedge policy was debated at city council meetings leading up to the general election. At one, statements on the traditions of American townscape, the beauty of Latin-inspired courtyard housing, the sanctity of green lawns—in short a compendium of design logics—were introduced into the record. Several councilpersons apologized for their and the city's culpability in fanning the controversy and further resolved to develop new guidelines for hedges. Notwithstanding this gesture, Shriver was the top vote getter in the 2004 election, changing the political landscape of the council and in the near future, no doubt, the landscape features of this city.

Santa Monica hedges, the Americana at Brand, and the expansion of LAX—what these situations have in common is the intensity and comprehensiveness of their associated public planning discourse. No doubt this intensity is in part an expression of both fear of change and a desire to preserve myopic and selfish interests. But the exhaustiveness of the processes described does not allow narrowly drawn interests to survive. In each case, a broad range of constituencies and interest groups considers a wide array of ideas in full public view. Decisions and consequent design are debated and crafted by citizens acting as design and planning experts. Ideas, indeed design ideas, mutate and coalesce through either the threat of a direct vote or a pending vote. Democracy, in which "the people form a master that must be obeyed," once again takes command of the design of neighborhoods, streets, the city, and the region.

This democratic planning and design process, far from being ad hoc, is increasingly institutionalized through new layers of mandated public input. Voters in the City of Los Angeles have recently approved two means to facilitate public planning review. The first, a network of city-sanctioned neighborhood councils, was an outcome of a 1999 voter-approved change to the city charter. Charter reform also spawned the new Department of Neighborhood Empowerment (DONE), which oversees self-organizing neighborhood councils that are locally elected and partially funded by the city. While the neighborhood councils are only advisory, they do have mandates to comment on all planning, development, and design issues. While the power to comment without the power to approve is limiting, the existence of their mandate shapes council debates and decision making. The viewpoints of the neighborhood councils, given their propensity to highlight alternative approaches and breed visible leadership challenges if their viewpoints are ignored, keep elected decision makers listening, coordinating, and cooperating.

Los Angeles has also created a stew of public planning checks and balances. Dozens of advisory boards oversee specific plans, historic preservation zones, community design districts, and specialized overlay zones throughout the city. Where these plans are in effect, all but the smallest projects are reviewed at open meetings for a wide array of use, bulk, and general design criteria. Many of these boards pass their work products to the neighborhood councils; democratic micro-incrementalism results. Power is distributed. No one group has the ability to realize unreasonable demands. The net result is an organized planning filter that in aggregate is bending the development and design direction of the city. Individual developers and home owners may bemoan the process when they are caught in its web, but so far the voters, as well as many pragmatic politicians, seem perfectly content to arrive at a regional definition of the good city through a consciously conversational system that micromanages from the bottom up.

The Rise of the Citizen Expert

One result of the public's insistent micromanagement of urban production in Los Angeles is additional physical fragmentation. Small is indeed beautiful. Yet this is a different type of small than the 1960s Jane Jacobs or the 1970s ecological versions. If those were based on an efficacy formed by Modernism—smaller is healthier—today's small is dominated by quests for personal convenience, safety, and comfort. This again parallels an evolution of the landscape anticipated by Tocqueville, who suggested that democratic nations will "cultivate the arts that serve to render life easy."[2]

When Tocqueville was writing, information about what shaped city design was either nonexistent or accessible to a few. In a digital age, the democratization of planning is accelerated through ever-increasing availability of information that laypersons use to interpret and manage the impacts of projects. For instance, at LAX, citizen groups pour over noise studies that measure the effect of moving the runway fifty feet south. Or in Glendale, alternative designs, real estate pro formas, and tax increment projections accompanied electioneering for and against the Americana. With the capacity to view information comes the ability to micromanage planning from the public dais or voting booth. This does slow the development and design of urbanism to a crawl. Yet despite the sluggish pace, inexorably Los Angeles mass transit gets built, the Los Angeles River reimagined, storm sewer systems constructed, master planned developments projected, and ten of thousands of housing units erected. With all this, it is easy to overlook the most critical infrastructure being formed: the participatory planning frameworks that consume the statistics, weigh the alternatives, and direct the shape of Los Angeles's urbanism.

In this environment, the planning discourses of everyday life and professional plans for the form of the metropolis gradually become one. "Everyday" people are asked to consume and form opinions about everything from large-scale infrastructural decisions to tot lot beautification. Information is posted online and citizens—particularly those that are obsessed—know that armed with these data they too can be experts. Even with the consequent focus on the local and the self-interested, this process nevertheless sets up the planner to play a key facilitation and brokering role. This is not easy given the microscopic viewpoint of much of the citizenry, but it is possible, even as it demands new planning practices and frameworks, in essence the construction of a "New Planning" for consensus building and decision making.

Collaborative Planning and L.A.'s Urbanity

The more the process of creating the look and feel of Los Angeles becomes subject to an institutionalized and multilayered discourse, the better this landscape gets, the less it is a "blank." This is not Pollyannaish optimism. Since I moved to Los Angeles in 1985, the air has become cleaner, there are more good places to hang out, historic preservation has become a fact, not an aberration, innovations of national importance such as the introduction of bus rapid transit have been adopted, and mixed-use projects are reinventing the look and feel of suburban commercial strips. On the present agenda of the city are grassroots demands for inclusionary housing and the reclamation of the Los Angeles River. Ten years after voters banned further construction of below-grade fixed-rail subways, advocacy groups and a smattering of local politicians are even calling for the construction of new underground lines, a seemingly apostate L.A. position that has been calmly received—all this progress even where the driver is supposedly NIMBYism.

Under these conditions, Los Angeles is accepting an urban cast. Reyner Banham's sunshine-filled suburban sprawl of freeways, beaches, mountains, single-family houses, and middle-class desires, as defined in his *Los Angeles: The Architecture of the Four Ecologies,* is slowly fading. A new generation wants walkable urban experiences and a mix of dwelling types in neighborhoods. They are willing to ride public transit and even believe in public schools (over the past ten years voters in Los Angeles have consistently approved bond measures that now add up to billions of dollars for construction of new schools). Their fears about the limits of acceptable urbanization are, of course, always present.

Southern Californians in general continue to resist overarching regional and metropolitan place making. Nevertheless alternative urban models and planning knowledge are emerging—particularly those of New Urbanism—and are widely distributed by planning officials and citizens seeking alternatives to sprawl. The New Urbanist model provides an unambiguous tool for starting discussions regarding urban density and form, mass transit, city- and town-based lifestyles, and even abstract policy choices such as those concerning the subregional balance between jobs and housing. Yet, the amalgam that increasingly forms the look and feel of contemporary Los Angeles stretches the definition of any found model or ideology. Angelenos want their urban villages. They also want their freeways. What comes to be is a Los Angeles urbanism made up of a little bit of this and a little bit of that.

In Southern California, textbook planning that promotes an idyllic landscape of neatly separated villages clustered about downtown-like concentrations of mixed-use development, all integrated with fixed-rail transit—indeed any type of rationalized and smoothly efficient urban system—are run through the grinder of public process and always end up looking and functioning differently and better than originally imagined. The recently opened master-planned beachside community of Playa Vista and new infill development in downtown Los Angeles demonstrate this point. At Playa Vista, the planning efforts of New Urbanism's elite, millions of dollars of planning expenditures, and city regulation that sought to codify master-plan intentions have culminated in the creation of a "town within a town" as well as the restoration of one of the last wetlands along the regional coastline. On paper this result bespeaks success, yet it was not developers, planners, or designers but citizen opponents who worked their way through a twenty-year public review process and lawsuits that finally encouraged the state to intervene, purchase the signature feature of the development—a park constituting half the site—and force the restoration of both fresh and saltwater marshes.

Meanwhile in downtown Los Angeles—an environment full of never-completed, if not quite foiled, urban renewal projects—tweaks of the building code relieving parking and fire requirements that were long demanded by preservation groups and development interests helped usher in the adaptive reuse of dozens of older and historic buildings. With the changes in regulation, a 10,000-unit building-by-building residential rehabilitation boom occurred within the confines of the central city. Dwarfing Playa Vista's 5,800 projected units, this boom at first seems an unmitigated planning success. Yet like Playa Vista this most recent downtown renaissance involved twenty years of hard work and endless conversations, dialogues with developers and property owners, occasional lawsuits by preservationists, and the input of politicians and public officials who believed that the premises of downtown redevelopment focused too heavily on the new.

Even with success that demonstrates the development leverage achievable through incremental approaches, planning proceeds on two old-school mega-redevelopment projects in downtown. One of these projects is adjacent to Disney Hall, the other integrated with the downtown sports arena, Staples Center. Both will reportedly feature internally oriented "experiences." Given that these projects will be constrained by the voice of the recently formed Downtown

Neighborhood Council, a relationship to context will likely be grafted, if not forced, on both. The most likely end result will be a hybrid, neither this nor that, and thereby consistent with the larger emerging Los Angeles urban landscape.

To further the potential of this hyper-incremental planning dialogue, the most important infrastructure that needs to be improved in Los Angeles, indeed in most cities, is the process itself, making it more efficient and providing that it is inclusive of many viewpoints—both of which the City of Los Angeles is working to address. The Department of Neighborhood Empowerment now sponsors an ongoing Neighborhood Empowerment Academy and once-a-year neighborhood congresses in which all the councils gather, meet with elected officials, discuss the issues, and seek to better organize their processes and learn from their failures as well as their successes. After an initial rush of neighborhood council formation in communities where interest was high, the city also found that to ensure inclusiveness, it needed to make a concerted effort to seed councils in poorer neighborhoods and communities of color that did not initially self-organize. At this point, five years after the organizing began, the city is almost completely blanketed by active councils.

Regardless of the increased means for local input, too many people still do not participate. Lack of participation is in part the result of cynicism about the potential of politics in general and local planning politics in particular, particularly when implementation takes so long. Lack of input may also be due to the fact that people's lives are busier than ever. The number of issues that get vetted at simultaneous meeting opportunities is vast. There are simply too many meetings. Long-term success for the neighborhood councils may depend on their ability to usurp the need for so many overlapping efforts. The city will have to make a concerted effort to channel most public planning discourse toward the councils, thereby increasing their profile and role. In essence, the neighborhood councils have to become the modern day equivalents of the New England town meetings Tocqueville observed 175 years ago. With over ninety councils formed (in a city with only fifteen council districts), increased participation is guaranteed. The large number of geographically dispersed councils now ensures that a wider range of viewpoints will emerge, lessening the potential for one group or type of stakeholder to dominate.

New Roles for Planners and Designers

If eliciting a broad spectrum of public input leads incrementally to better urban form, then planners and designers will need to participate in more of the events (and, properly, be paid to do so) that people are already attending—not only the neighborhood council meetings but also the school meetings, church events, local festivals, and block parties constantly on the calendar of daily life. The resources demanded for this enterprise need to be understood as equivalent in importance, if not in fiscal impact, to infrastructural projects like airport expansions, downtown revitalizations, or even the proper height of hedge rows. Promoting the development of the infrastructure of process in turn suggests new opportunities for planners, additional roles for architects and landscape architects, and challenges for urban designers.

As the advocacy models of the 1960s lost their currency in the 1970s and 1980s, planners were increasingly reduced to performing the driest forms of zoning and land-use entitlement administration. By the 1990s, one heard, at least among some architects, that planning was dead.[3] Today, with the need to manage the collection and interpretation of data, administer and facilitate ongoing public processes, and generate policy in response to public demands, planning again assumes a central role in the development process. In essence, planning has evolved from a generalist's occupation that sought to lead people to environmentally based solutions—utilize a bit of physical design, sprinkle it with a bit of law, and spice with facilitation—to a highly specialized and demanding profession that partners with communities to manage the complex ins and outs of a transparent and public development process. That this process is often confusing and contradictory reinforces the idea that planners are needed to better manage the assumed discursive process.

Interestingly, as the process becomes more conversational, visual representation and physical design are once again becoming key tools of planning. As the public demands more information about alternative futures and accessible means to understand the data, planners are increasingly using digital software and visualization to allow real-time explorations of the relationships between social, environmental, economic, and land-use data with built form proposals. Newer GIS-based programs, such as CommunityViz,[4] allow walk-throughs of prospective environments. Building envelopes as well as cityscapes can be instantaneously related to an endless menu of criteria such as vehicle trips generated, optimal energy utilization, or desired tax streams. For the first time since the 1930s, planning is becoming more form based. With these tools, planners are able to bypass the design professions at the conceptual stages of projects. It is just a matter of time before planners themselves are bypassed by compulsive citizens who will insist on playing the virtual planning game, much as they already play Sim City. Still, the citizenry that is willing to manipulate the simulator will need active and ongoing support—planners will play the role of expert assistants.

With the new visualization tools, architects and landscape architects may no longer be the natural leaders for the conceptualization of planning ideas. However, as demands for visualization increase, they too, like planners, will play key support roles in the New Planning. Professional designers will maintain a deeper knowledge and understanding of the relationships between planning conceptualization and the craft and science of physical construction. A continuing need will exist to integrate the knowledge and experience of licensed professionals of building systems, codes, life-safety issues, and construction execution into the process of citizen-based generation of visual urban alternatives. While overlap exists between landscape architecture and architecture, each profession also has a specific history and legal responsibilities separate from planning or citizen processes. The design professions can maintain a contributory role within the public planning process. What is not as clear is the place of urban design.

Urban design, as a perusal of most urban design curricula will confirm, remains committed to imparting general knowledge about law, planning, real estate economics, and design of places to engender urban sociability. The expectation is that graduating students, with their ability to see the big picture, are the obvious people to make critical connections and lead design and planning efforts. Yet much of what urban design promised when it was formulated in the mid-1950s and now imparts at increasing numbers of programs—mainly the need to make places and buildings that respect the synergies of the street, neighborhood, and city—is now accepted knowledge that laypeople, at least in Los Angeles, understand and act on. These people do not need urban designers to advocate these ideas for them. Urban designers cannot continue to be educated as generalists—in fact urban design as a professional pursuit is in crisis—when the activist layperson's understanding of the city and how to act within it is equivalent to the purported professional's.

For designers who would be urbanists, the challenge is to move beyond the general knowledge of citizens engaged in planning their communities. The future of urban design now lies in the development and use of information systems and tools that all players in the community-making process will use. Understanding and supporting these knowledge bases and tools so they are integral parts of the democratic planning process are one of the great opportunities for the planning and design professions and portend a shift of historic proportions with regard to the means by which cities are planned, designed, and built, a shift as important as the design of any piece of infrastructure. As opposed to advocating urban design education for the masses or leading the people to the city on the hill of good design, planners, architects, and landscape architects, acting as urban designers, must associate themselves and their specialized activities with everyday people to do everyday planning.

Gropingly, the public in Los Angeles has already used this nascent process, this New Planning, to get cleaner air, cleaner water, better traffic management, less development intrusion into single-family house neighborhoods, greener streets, better designed projects, and more vital urbanism in select locations. However, the challenge is also qualitative, highlighting another dilemma for the generalist urban designer. Quantitative expertise, good planning processes, and generalized knowledge of urban design do not ensure the production of good, innovative, or progressive urban environments. What does are the details of design that citizen experts never draw, that planners necessarily abstract, and that urban designers, if not expert in design implementation, defer to architects and landscape architects, who remain the professionals that best integrate citizen-based planning concerns and practices into the actual bricks and mortar of qualitative place making. The challenge of the New Planning for urban "designers" is that it insists that they remain first and foremost creators and makers of urban environments.

Tocqueville noted that Americans "habitually prefer the useful to the beautiful."[5] Perhaps this explains well the sense that much of the Los Angeles landscape, indeed the American landscape, has been exploited to the point of permanent degradation. In opposition to processes that led to an overemphasis on the useful, we now see in democratic planning situations a consciousness that calls for the beautiful as well as the useful. Both criteria now guide Los Angeles toward a planning process that needs the knowledge and skills of architects and landscape architects as integral elements in citizen-based decision making. With both criteria operational, these professionals again have a clear role, not only as the designers of urban landmarks but also as substantive contributors to the never-ending planning and design debates in the always evolving everyday city.

Notes

1. "Democracy not only leads men to a vast number of inconsiderable productions; it also leads them to raise some monuments on the largest scale; but between these two extremes there is a blank." Alexis de Tocqueville, *Democracy in America,* vol. 2 (1835; New York: Vintage, 1990), 53.

2. Ibid., 48.

3. Thom Mayne, who is known for his strong and heartfelt commentary, has stated to me on several occasions that there is no planning. Rem Koolhaas has surely also advocated a version of this argument. The gentler version of this critique, mainly that there is no planning despite the presence of it as an activity in municipal government, was long the topic of conversation during the time I actively participated in the Urban Design Committee of the Los Angeles Chapter of the American Institute of Architects.

4. See www.communityviz.com.

5. Tocqueville, *Democracy in America,* 48.

4 Can Planning Be a Means to Better Architecture? Chicago's Building Boom and Design Quality

Lynn Becker

In Chicago, planning and superior design are on parallel paths that seldom converge. Regional planning has largely lost interest in the quality of the built environment, and municipal regulation of new construction, by its charge, is less a force for extending Chicago's legacy of architectural innovation than a machine for maximizing development while merely taming the most egregious design failings offered up by the market economy. As a result, seldom in Chicago's history has the will to create superior architecture been as marginalized as it is today. Let me explain.

Daniel Burnham placed architectural design at the center of his 1909 *Plan of Chicago*. Today, mention of the plan is most likely to evoke not its ideas but instead Jules Guerin's stunning renderings of districts composed of new buildings sharing a uniform cornice height, standardized massing, and generic French Empire detailing. Probably its most famous image is of a gargantuan city hall that looked forward less to Mies van der Rohe than to Albert Speer.

Fast forward to nearly a century later. The Commercial Club of Chicago, the same organization that commissioned Burnham's plan, issues *Chicago Metropolis 2020: Preparing Metropolitan Chicago for the 21st Century*. There isn't a single illustration in the entire 120-page document.[1]

To the authors of this document, "The Burnham Plan, in an economically burgeoning era, focused on the theme of beauty."[2] The new plan, in contrast, is all about process: education, land use, transportation, and, above all, jobs. The actual physical form the future might take doesn't seem to be worth speculation. For architecture, the dominant reality of our time is the triumph of a market economy increasingly dependent on converting products, services, ideas, and even the components of the built environment into lower-cost, easily reproducible commodities. Planning is, almost by definition, an insult to such pure market economics.

In the real world, of course, only zealots are pure planners or free-market disciples. Especially in Chicago, which could be said to be the city of the deal. "Politics ain't beanbag," Finley Peter Dunne's Mr. Dooley said in the 1890s, reflecting a disdain for reformers that lives on in the city to this day.[3] Planners are reformers at their worst, and the more far-reaching their plans have been, the easier they have been to ignore or suborn.

It is hard to think of an architect who was more of an equal among the city's power brokers than Burnham, but Chicago—and its architecture—still developed along a quite different path than his plan intended. Even when his vision *was* realized, it was often in the context of diminution and unexpected consequences. The plan's recommended building of a bridge across the river in 1922 *did* transform grubby Pine Street, renamed North Michigan Avenue, into the city's elite boulevard, but it also set the stage, later in the 1970s, for "Boul Mich" to replace State Street as Chicago's primary retailing strip and to leave what was for over a century the city's essential economic engine a dilapidated and needy presence. Burnham's grand domed civic center never stood a chance. Envisioned as the centerpiece for a relocated heart of the city about a mile west of the Loop, it is the site today of the "spaghetti bowl"—three converging expressways and the arcing, elevated ramps that connect them. A Gordian knot of barrier and disruption, it has, for over four decades, successfully repulsed any idea of restoring the continuity of the surrounding urban fabric.

Planning is a lot better at coming to grips with the immediate past than it is at predicting and shaping the future. When Burnham created his 1909 plan, he was responding to an explosive, anarchic city that since 1880 had added a million and a half inhabitants and quadrupled in acreage—congested, unsanitary, and often lawless acreage.

His remedy drew heavily on the previous century's example of Haussmann's Paris, carving broad boulevards through the maze of medieval streets to ease circulation and creating parks that would provide citizens a gentler outlet for social impulses that could turn disruptive or even violent in the older, overcrowded city.

After 1909, Chicago would continue to grow explosively, adding over a half million people in each of the next two decades, filling out the farmlands at the edge of the city, and reaching a peak 3,620,000 people in the 1950 census. What followed, however, was not the consolidating urbanism that Burnham optimistically projected but a brief plateau followed by precipitous decline.

One of the key conduits of that decline was the modern rethinking of the 1909 plan's broad boulevards. Burnham's plan consolidated the city's twenty-two trunk lines to alleviate the way the railroads sliced up the city, but in the 1950s that lesson was quickly forgotten in the rush to embrace the emerging culture of the automobile and tap into the public works funds that the federal government was making available to link U.S. cities through the creation of an interstate highway system. Now it was new expressways that plowed through neighborhoods and split them apart. More perversely, while the railroads built up Chicago's population, the new expressways functioned as a siphon, sucking panicky middle-class whites out of the city to be replaced by exploited minorities and expanding blight. By the 1990 census, the city's population density, defined by persons per square mile, had declined 30 percent from its 1950 peak. Beyond the glittering towers of the 1950s, 1960s, and 1970s designed by Mies and his followers, the city was hollowing out. Planning in the 1950s and 1960s set the stage for Chicago's becoming a negative doppelganger of the new suburban utopia.

Neighborhoods just blocks south or west of the Loop were in steep decline. In the South Loop, the Printers Row district had been abandoned by the industry in favor of new plants in the suburbs. A twenty-two-story skyscraper, the 1911 Transportation Building, sat empty and abandoned. Chicago architect Harry Weese took note of the shabby, slablike hulk from the window of an airplane as it flew over the city, and he thought of his daughter's story about the lofts in New York's SoHo district that had found new life converted into apartments. By 1981, Weese had teamed with Lawrence Booth, another key Chicago architect, to create over two hundred housing units in the Transportation Building's homely shell. It was the beginning of Chicago's back-to-the-city movement, to be followed by the conversion of additional loft structures and the building of the new community of Dearborn Park on the abandoned railroad yards leading into the now restored Dearborn Station.

This new movement would continue to percolate largely under the radar until the economic boom of the 1990s, when it would roar into the foreground with an explosion of construction. Thirty-two thousand housing units were added downtown from 1980 to 2001—more than in any other city, with still another fifteen thousand created between 2000 and 2002.[4] Huge developments like Central Station were created on former rail yards. Residential conversions of historic industrial lofts, coupled with new residential towers, have transformed the long-derelict districts on the Loop's periphery into thriving communities. In outlying neighborhoods, old courtyard buildings have been upgraded and converted into condominiums, while new townhouse developments have sprouted like mushrooms, often in the form of teardowns of the historic homes and cottages that gave the neighborhoods their character. The bulk of this development has taken place outside any planning process remotely like Burnham's 1909 blueprint.

This is also arguably the first building boom in memory fueled not by prestige office towers designed by internationally regarded architects but by increasingly generic condo towers, the residential equivalent of the warehouse store. The goodies inside—in this case the floor plans, the appliances, the views—are what is important. Spending money on the wrapper is not.

In the revised Chicago skyline, the isolated examples of great Chicago design—Lucien LaGrange's spiky, glass-walled Erie on the Park, Ralph Johnson's airy split-towered Skybridge, and Jean-Paul Viguier's Sofitel Water Tower hotel, which reinvents the Chicago skyscraper with French elegance, Corbusian geometry, and a bit of Morris Lapidus—struggle not to be overwhelmed by the tidal wave of forty-, fifty-, and even sixty-story mediocrities, constructed of poured concrete, with a perfunctory sense of massing, and ugly above-grade garages that cling to the lot line and turn surrounding streets into dead canyons.

Like learning in the Dark Ages, architecture of the type that won Chicago world renown has largely withdrawn into the cloisters of academia. Just last year, striking new buildings by Rem Koolhaas and Helmut Jahn opened on the IIT campus. At the University of Chicago are Cesar Pelli's brawny Ratner Athletic Center and new dorms by Ricardo Legorreta. This fall, Rafael Viñoly's University of Chicago Graduate School of Business opened just across the street from Frank Lloyd Wright's Robie House, which is reflected in the boxed massing of its new, far-larger neighbor, just as the flaring cylindrical columns of Viñoly's winter garden evoke both the dominant Gothic traditions of the campus architecture and Wright's own flaring lily pad columns in the Johnson Wax Building. You will not find the names of any of these architects on any of the residential towers in downtown Chicago. The same free-market economics that fueled the city's turn-of-the-twenty-first-century boom has proved that you can sell a lot of condos without caring much about architectural quality.

The city of Chicago's priority in all this seems to have been getting every last drop of development on the tax roles and dealing with the consequences only after they became fact. It was not until this past year, after most of the building and most of the damage had been done, that the city got around to finalizing a new Central Area Plan (CAP), which codifies the already operational concept of moving new office development to a location away from the Loop, west of the Chicago River. While macroplans like the CAP tend to get all the press, it is the microplans, in the form of municipal regulation, that are the ones with an actual direct effect on what gets built. Unlike the sugar plum visions of the big-picture planners, zoning and building codes tell developers in often dizzying detail exactly what they can do and what they cannot. Rewrites of both the zoning and building codes have recently been finalized.

The new zoning ordinance went into effect on November 1, 2004. It seeks to address many of the failings of the recent crop of residential towers. There are floor-area ratio bonuses for placing parking below grade and for wrapping above-grade parking with occupiable space. Other design flaws are addressed with highly specific mandates: "Large expanses of blank walls should be avoided. . . . If solid windowless walls are necessary . . . they should be articulated with arches, piers, columns, planters," and so on.[5] Such prescriptions, however well intended, are less incentives to great design than invitations to a pervasive banality.

It often appears that Chicago's most creative new buildings are those with the lightest bureaucratic oversight. The zoning ordinance categorizes any project that crosses set thresholds of height or density as "planned developments," subject to an intensified scrutiny that adds a preliminary hearing held by the city's Plan Commission to the usual process of review by the zoning and planning departments, followed by a city council hearing and final action by the council as whole. All of the worst new towers are planned developments. Two of the best—Erie on the Park and Ralph Johnson's new Contemporaine—are not.

When vetting new proposals for development, the city's Department of Planning and Development largely sticks to resolving zoning compliance issues before passing projects on to the Plan Commission, which must approve them before they are sent on to the city council. The commission also sees its role in mitigating bad design as limited. The emphasis is more on traffic control and the life of the street. With the recent additions to the building ordinance, the new hope is that even bad buildings will be forced to contribute to a more lively and livable streetscape. The bottom line, however, in the words of architect Linda Searl, is that "you can't make an architect or developer do a better building."[6] Searl is acting chair of the Plan Commission. Although the last chair left over six months ago, the mayor has yet to name a replacement.[7]

Many members of the commission seem almost starved for superior, contemporary design. Reacting to architect Ron Krueck's bold glass-faceted design for a new Spertus Museum as it came up for consideration at a recent meeting, Doris Holleb's comment about "welcoming a design that doesn't hearken back to the late part of the nineteenth century" was only one of several remarks from commissioners that appeared to signal an impatience with the faux classicism of an architect like Lucien LaGrange, who likes to top off his luxury condo towers with mansard roofs whose execution in painted metal evokes the Quonset hut as much as the French Second Empire.[8]

This is the same LaGrange whose firm also designed Erie on the Park. The difference in quality derives less from any kind of planning or regulatory intervention than from the identity of the developer. A handful of developers, such as Smithfield Properties' Bill Smith, responsible for both Erie and its striking neighbor Kingsbury on the Park, also by LaGrange, and Colin Kinhke of CMK Development (the Contemporaine), account for a disproportionate amount of new, innovative design.

The role of Mayor Daley remains an enigma. "No More Ugly Buildings" was the headline he provided the *Chicago Sun-Times* early in 2003.[9] His energetic championing of the ultramodern work of Frank

Gehry and others in the city's new Millennium Park, a refuge of creativity within an increasingly generic city, would appear to confirm a receptiveness to modern design. Several trips to Paris left him with a deepened awareness of the importance of superior urban design and an increased commitment to bringing those lessons home to Chicago, but, as in a game of "telephone," his intentions have tended to become garbled by the time they reach the end of the communications chain. For years the word on the street was that Daley favored retro–Beaux Arts design, and the result can be seen in all those mansard-topped buildings and in the Art Nouveau feel of the heavy black lines of Robert A. M. Stern's bus shelters. Did Daley tell the architects that's what he wanted? Probably not. More likely, the designs were the result of planners' and architects' self-censoring, trying to anticipate what would please the prince.

The bottom line is that exceptional design is both subjective and, more importantly from a design standpoint, intangible. That is undoubtedly one of the reasons the mayor has found the idea of promoting Chicago as the "the greenest city in America" so compelling. Not only is sustainable architecture widely accepted as a desirable goal, but also it can be measured and documented. There is even an organization, the Green Building Council, keeping score, awarding LEED certifications—silver, gold, and platinum—in a sort of green architecture Olympics. The city has formulated a "Chicago Standard" to create LEED-certified buildings that will reduce energy costs 15 to 20 percent. The Twenty-second District Police Station, which opened in June 2004, was designed to attain a LEED Silver rating.[10] That is a lot easier to put into a press release than trying to explain why a certain new building is a superior design.

The Burnham Plan tried to imagine the look of the future and succeeded only in reflecting the architecture of the past. Perhaps it is only fitting, therefore, that faced with the same issue a century later, the *Chicago Metropolis 2020* plan decided it just didn't want to get involved.

Local architects and institutions have tried to fill in the gaps. In December 2004, the Art Institute of Chicago opened a new exhibition, Chicago Architecture: Ten Visions,[11] that includes highly imaginative proposals for the city's future from ten of its leading architects, including an installation by Chicago architect Douglas Garofalo that uses student design projects to "illuminate" ideas in the image-free *Chicago Metropolis 2020* plan.

That none of these proposals in this and similar past shows now has any shot of morphing into a real project exposes the soft underbelly of promoting design excellence in Chicago. The city itself has sponsored several architectural competitions but to date none has translated into construction.

Chicago is not an island. Its successes and failures derive, as they do throughout the country, from the forces of today's largely unfettered free-market economy. In the larger metro area, what is going on in Chicago is almost a sideshow. The Northern Illinois Planning Council projects that over 80 percent of the region's population growth through 2030 will occur outside of the City of Chicago.[12] The architecture of America's center cities may be what is most visible, but it is the architecture of urban sprawl that continues to dominate, confounding the best intentions of planners.

Not that long ago, every city and most towns had their own First National Bank, inevitably housed in a structure designed to express its singular sense of importance. It was just one of a range of numerous institutions in retailing, entertainment, and commerce, locally based, that depended on architecture to express a distinctive personality. Today, an ever-smaller number of ever-larger corporations supplant localized presence with standardized architectural prototypes, infinitely reproducible. If we don't think twice about shopping in warehouses as long they can provide the goods we want at a more affordable price, why should we be any less comfortable living in generic towers—the vertical equivalent of the big-box retailer—if the spaces they enclose bring the comforts we desire within our economic reach?

Planning, despite its sometimes-utopian connotations, does not change who we are. At the moment, most of us remain creatures of a free-market economy in which superior architecture has become almost a boutique endeavor, isolated from its mainstream impulses. And if you are inclined to retort that this has always been true, think again. It was not true during the time of the first Chicago School, many of whose masterpieces are simple loft buildings, commodities prepared on tight budgets. Nor was it true in the second Chicago School of Mies and his followers, where a big-ticket project almost always meant design by a top architect.

To repeat: seldom in Chicago's history has the will to create superior architecture been as marginalized as it is today. Planning, best at fixing past mistakes and trying to prevent their recurrence, cannot reverse the trend. Its most basic power is proscriptive, not creative. It is actually most likely to stand in the way of truly innovative designs that use emerging technology to create new solutions that wind up being dramatically different from those we are used to—those that planning is most comfortable enforcing.

When Chicago's Millennium Park started out, it consisted of a parking garage topped by parkland designed by Skidmore, Owings, and Merrill in a traditional Beaux Arts style.[13] That was the scope of the planning apparatus's vision: cover railroad tracks just off Michigan Avenue that had been an open ditch for over a century, rebuild a parking garage so that its revenue covered the costs of the bonds, and give the public a new park with the comforting look of Daniel Burnham and Edward Bennett's original Grant Park designs. Practical, fiscally responsible, and architecturally embalmed.

Millennium Park, Chicago, Illinois, 2004. Photograph courtesy of Terry Evans, Revealing Chicago.

Then Chicago's Pritzkers, the family behind the Nobel-scaled Pritzker prize for architecture, got involved, setting the wheels in motion for engaging Frank Gehry to design the park's new band shell.[14] Once Gehry was in place, the project exploded exponentially in ambition and daring (and cost, both public and private, to a final tab of just under a half billion dollars).[15] By the time Millennium Park opened in July 2004, it had become a bold speculation on the power of modern design to reinvent the urban environment.

Planning consolidates and conserves; only ego, restless and voracious, creates.

Notes

1. Elmer W. Johnson, *Chicago Metropolis 2020: Preparing Chicago for the 21st Century* (Chicago: Commercial Club of Chicago, January 1999), www.chicagometropolis2020.org/plan.pdf; accessed January 6, 2005.

2. Johnson, *Chicago Metropolis 2020,* 4.

3. Finley Peter Dunne, *Mr. Dooley in Peace and War,* reprint ed. (Champaign: University of Illinois Press, 2001), xxv.

4. Chicago Central Area Plan, City of Chicago, June 12, 2003, chapter 2, 21; available at http://egov.cityofchicago.org.

5. Chicago Zoning Ordinance, Section 17-8, Planned Developments, 8, 9.

6. Interview with Linda Searl, December 17, 2004.

7. David Roeder, "High-Rise Hotels in View for Wacker Drive Parcel," *Chicago Sun-Times,* December 12, 2004, 89.

8. Personal notes from November 18, 2004, meeting of the Chicago Plan Commission.

9. David Roeder and Fran Spielman, "Daley: No More Ugly Buildings, Demands Developers Stay on the 'Cutting Edge,'" *Chicago Sun-Times,* February 16, 2005, 1.

10. See http://egov.cityofchicago.org; accessed January 6, 2005.

11. www.artic.edu/aic/exhibitions/10visions/home.html; January 6, 2005.

12. www.nipc.org/2030_forecast_endorsed_093003.htm#Northeastern; accessed January 5, 2005.

13. Allen Freeman, "Fair Game on Lake Michigan," *Landscape Architecture,* November 2004, as viewed at www.asla.org/lamag/lam04/november/feature3.html; accessed December 21, 2004.

14. Kevin Nance, "Pritzker Pavilion: 'A Sculpture, Not Just a Building,'" *Chicago Sun-Times,* July 11, 2004, 4.

15. Liam Ford, "How a Budget Tripled in Six Years," *Chicago Tribune,* July 15, 2004, 13.

5

An Anatomy of Civic Ambition in Vancouver: Toward Humane Density

Leonie Sandercock

Vancouver's Vertical Miracle

In their devastating 2003 critique of transportation megaprojects, subtitled *An Anatomy of Ambition*, Bent Flyvbjerg, Nils Bruzelius, and Werner Rothengatter demonstrate (as does Flyvbjerg alone in his essay in this volume) the systematic overemphasis of public benefits and underestimation of costs, the lies and deceptions designed to thwart the public interest, that typically characterize such projects.[1] In contrast to their noir exposé, the story I am about to unfold about Vancouver's downtown residential megaprojects since the late 1980s is one of stunning success, a demonstration of how and why "good" is possible in planning, and how the regulation of urban form and urban design can create better cities.

In the late 1980s, the City of Vancouver embarked on a large downtown urban redevelopment project that flew in the face of conventional wisdom in North America. Against the prevailing "suburban ideal" of low-density, single-family housing as the dominant residential development form, or the emerging, "back to the future" New Urbanism, Vancouver's planners believed they could attract people to the central city and create a vibrant, mixed-use downtown by developing high-density, high-rise residential precincts on vacant industrial lands. Working closely with developers, architects, and urban designers, these planners aimed to produce high-quality residential neighborhoods and, simultaneously, major amenities for the Vancouver public. Now hailed

Stanley Park, across harbor from Vancouver, 1991. Photograph copyright Annie Griffiths Belt/Corbis.

as "the Vancouver Miracle" or, more demurely, "the Vancouver Achievement," Vancouver's fastest-growing residential downtown in North America has now piqued the interest of developers and planners worldwide.[2]

Almost 40,000 people have moved downtown within the past ten years, occupying the more than 150 high-rises that have sprouted within a mile radius of the central business district (CBD). Eighty thousand people now live in the downtown peninsula, a figure expected to rise to 120,000 by 2020. This densification of downtown has helped make the Greater Vancouver metropolitan region about 100 percent denser than Seattle.[3] But this new urban forest of glass and steel is also a city of neighborhoods, of green, of mixed-use, of schools, shops, and community centers, of twenty kilometers of continuous seawall for public recreational use encircling downtown, and, arguably, of the highest-quality urban public realm in North America. How was all this possible?

Historical and Institutional Background: A Civic Revolt

The City of Vancouver, with a population in 2004 of 583,000, is the historic core of what is now a metropolitan region of 2.1 million people.

As a municipality, the city enjoys unusual political and planning autonomy, thanks to the Vancouver Charter, granted by the province of British Columbia in 1953, which gave the city much greater powers of self-government than those of other Canadian cities, which remain subservient to provincial municipal acts. This has allowed the city council and the director of planning significant scope for policy innovation and direct response to local circumstances.

Until the early 1970s, Vancouver's urban development and planning history was on a trajectory much like that of other North American cities. There were massive high-rise redevelopments of the bad old kind in the West End neighborhood on the downtown peninsula throughout the 1960s, at the expense of historic housing; sprawling suburbs; and plans for a freeway system to bring commuters downtown, a system that would have cut through the heart of the low-income inner neighborhood of Strathcona. In response to the freeway threat and to the shock of West End redevelopment, citizens mobilized to present and protect a different vision of a more livable city.

By 1972, the pro-business Non-Partisan Association (NPA) party, which had dominated city politics, was ousted by a reform party (The Electors Action Movement, TEAM), which had a more sensitive approach to development, a more inclusive vision for the future of the city, and a more participatory planning process. TEAM was a short-lived municipal political party in the 1970s, one positioned between left and right at a time when reform movements were emerging across Canada in reaction to thoughtless development. The mayor, Art Phillips, was a millionaire businessman. Two University of British Columbia professors elected to this reform city council (a geographer and an architect) were influential in shaping a more environmentally and socially conscious approach, and in hiring a new director of planning, Ray Spaxman, who had established a reputation in Toronto as a planner sensitive to neighborliness and livability.

If there are heroes in the following story, they are the two directors of planning who have guided the city's reformed and unique discretionary planning system over the past three decades: Spaxman from 1973 to 1989 and his successor, Larry Beasley, director of Central Area planning since 1990 and co-director of planning since 1995. But there is far more to the story than two heroic planners/designers (as we shall see), and both men would insist that it has been the distinctive collaborative approach to planning across the city that is the central story. As Spaxman says, reflecting back on that period of change, "The individuals are not what is important; it is the team approach. The foresight of the Mayor of the time, together with the chair of the planning committee in the '70s, and the chair of the Planning Commission, and the Community Planning Association of the time, plus the mixture of reform-minded councilors and their political supporters, reflecting a newly recognized will of the people, are the people who made this happen."[4]

TEAM's planning agenda embraced neighborhood planning, affordable housing, heritage protection, and transit provision, but initially it was focused most on the improved control and better design of major development downtown. This involved reform of the development permit process, new plans and guidelines for downtown, an effective urban design policy, and heritage conservation initiatives. With Spaxman's arrival, work began immediately on an official development plan with a new set of development controls and design guidelines that John Punter describes as "a model of clear thinking."[5] At the end of 1974, the city council approved establishment of a three-person Development Permit Board, chaired by the director of planning. The board was to meet in public and keep minutes of its proceedings, thus giving transparency to its decisions.[6] The director of planning, as chair, had considerable power and influence.

First, the director was leader of a significant group of professionals in the Planning Department who were in the front line of developing new planning and design policies and who were the first to see early ideas from developers. The director was therefore both influential in the department and influenced by the department's advice. It would have been acknowledged by the "observing community" that the chair of the board, as also a voting member, had considerable influence on all development occurring in the city. (The "observing community" refers to those developers, architects, planners, politicians, citizens, and affected neighbors who were involved with the processes.) Spaxman, the chair of the Development Permit Board between 1974 and 1989, was enthusiastic about the benefits he believed would occur in development as a result of this new, transparent system. He was wholly committed to what he called "neighborliness" in development and design. The performance of the chair was entirely under public scrutiny and within well-articulated policies, guidelines, and processes that were debated at public meetings with all sides present. In the fifteen years that Spaxman was chair, there was not one occasion when the citizen, development industry, or urban design representatives or the three board members had a significant disagreement that needed to be referred to council. That level of harmony was, arguably, one of its major successes. Beasley, the current co-director of planning, continues to wield considerable influence and power, not as chair but as a voting member of the board.[7]

To work with this board, the council also approved an Urban Design Advisory Panel, made up of two representatives each from the development industry, the design professions, and the general public—this was another important move to create a more open and participatory process. The TEAM council thus brought into being a design-sensitive permitting system that has prompted commentators to describe Vancouver's approach as emphasizing urban design "in reshaping the city's structure, land use, and landscapes. Vancouver is distinguished by its sustained commitment to deploy civic powers and resources to reshape its urban space, form, and development trajectory."[8]

The decision of the TEAM council to transform the obsolete industrial landscape of False Creek South into a socially progressive, medium-density, mixed-income housing project (inspired by ideas of social mix as well as the design language of Christopher Alexander) signaled the new municipal commitment to inserting the public interest into the planning process, a commitment that has, with very few exceptions, characterized Vancouver's planning process since. But while the medium density of False Creek South in the 1970s was a response to the alarm caused by the insensitive high-rise redevelopment of the West End in the previous decade, descendants of the reform movement in subsequent decades again embraced the tower—a reimagined tower—as the form best suited to create a livable downtown.

After more than a decade of negotiation, the Central Area Plan, finally approved in 1991, did something remarkable in contemporary city-building history: In the context of a metropolitan regional growth management strategy that favored residential densification as the most sustainable way to accommodate future population growth, the plan abandoned the tentative efforts at growth management of the 1980s in favor of a strategic reallocation (and rezoning) of land in the downtown core, downsizing the office district within a consolidated CBD, thereby enabling and encouraging medium- to high-density housing throughout the rest of the downtown peninsula and inner city.[9] The public was enlisted as participants in these discourses, from neighborhood to neighborhood downtown, as plans were prepared for each of the major Central Area districts.

Since the mid-1980s, public discussion about a livable Central Area and the evolution of the new planning model was occurring at a time when Vancouver was emerging as a transnational city, driven largely by immigration and investment from the Asia-Pacific region, specifically Hong Kong. Local consensus has it that a turning point occurred in 1986, when Vancouver staged Expo 86, showcasing itself to the world and attracting the attention of wealthy and powerful Hong Kong developers. At this point, one might have expected the idealism of the 1970s to succumb to the forces of globalization, but that has not been so, as I will explain. It is to the post-Expo megaprojects that we now turn, to explore their success in local terms.

"The Vancouver Model": Megaprojects on the Waterfront

Expo 86 was sited on the north shore of False Creek, a swath of abandoned industrial land and railway yards. The province had acquired the land in the late 1970s from Canadian Pacific Railway and, shortly after Expo, decided to sell it. An international sale was organized, based on a financial bid and a concept design. Of three submitted proposals, the province selected that of Li Ka-Shing, Hong Kong's wealthiest developer, who wanted to provide his son Victor (an already established residential developer in the region) with a high-profile project to expand his capabilities, as well as to expand the Li family's property portfolio.[10] The purchase was a conspicuous demonstration of the globalization of the Vancouver economy and of Asian inroads into the city's property market.[11] And yet, as the seventy-six-hectare megaproject unfolded in coming years, the resulting built form and social outcomes did not at all represent a colonization of Vancouver's progressive planning principles. Why?

Unlike most waterfront megaprojects elsewhere, from London to Sydney,[12] those in Vancouver required no special legislation to override local planning provisions and processes to give developers what they wanted.[13] On the contrary, the long gestation process of the official development plan for False Creek North (FCN, also known as Concord Pacific, the name of the Li company handling this project) produced design principles (traceable in part to the False Creek South plan) that have shaped all subsequent residential megaprojects in Vancouver and that give the new vertical city its distinctive design, attractiveness of public realm, and attentiveness to social planning issues. It is important to note that all of the facilities and amenities in the following list of principles were intended to be covered (and have been) by the development cost levies and community amenity contributions paid by developers.

Punter summarizes these principles as:

- *Livable downtown neighborhoods*: proximity to downtown employment; high-net, medium-gross project density; social mix: 25 percent family housing, 20 percent social housing; livability: quiet, private, safe; offering views and amenities (see below); providing the public amenity of a seawall linking a system of parks.
- *Neighborhood facilities*: community centers, primary schools, and leisure facilities within each tower complex; park space; neighborhood shops and offices.
- *Livable streets*: extending the city grid to water's edge; eliminating through traffic (by designing narrow, neighborhood-scale streets); reducing on-street parking; creating pedestrian/bicycle streets, mews, and promenades with public art; making the public realm well-landscaped/furnished; integrating active commercial strips with the residential towers.
- *Generous park system*: regional parks for citywide use; differentiated functions: active/passive, for children/for adults, formal/informal; public seawall with thirty-five feet of public promenade, cycle, and sitting space; children's play space; neighborhood mini-parks.
- *Urban form*: townhouse and street-wall apartments; slim articulated tower and top;[14] perimeter blocks with green internal courtyards; clear gradations of public, semipublic, and private space; underground car parking.
- *Elevation treatment*: different designers for different precincts within the project; families of towers in each project; active street frontages: steps, porches, bays, balconies, patios; waterfront palette:[15] light colors and glass (these latter two elements achieve a sense of weightlessness and spaciousness unusual for high-rise precincts).[16]

Still, no matter how good the design principles were, it took a special local planning culture to ensure that these principles were implemented. Here, the detailed cooperative approach between city planners and developers already established under Spaxman and perfected by Beasley came into play in five years of meetings between city planners and the Concord Pacific design team, years that produced an accepted master plan for the site. Leading the Concord Pacific negotiating team was architect Stanley Kwok, who had been working in the city for fifteen years and "brought a new spirit of cooperation to the development side."[17]

This cooperative planning process is also unique to Vancouver. The emphasis is on collaboration by teams composed of developer and city staff to prepare master plans and convert them into official development plans, rezoning plans, and design guidelines, rather than on planners preparing concept plans on their own. The developer pays for the creation of a dedicated planning team to work full-time on project preparation, while the city works cooperatively, linking the planning function with other departments (Engineering, Social Planning, Parks) as necessary.[18] Over almost three decades, the evolution of this approach has socialized a new generation of talented designers into a civic-oriented design culture exceptional in North America, producing not only some excellent architecture and urban design (towers designed by James Cheng, Roger Hughes, Baker McGarva Hart, Busby Bridger, Paul Merrick, and others; market as well as social housing and award-winning parks by Richard Henriquez),[19] but also an outstanding urban public realm, defined in particular by the public spaces of the seawall itself, the parks strung along and connected by the seawall, and the public art in this area.

Again, unlike in waterfront megaprojects in other countries, here there was major public consultation during the intensive negotiation stage. Three different "publics" were identified by city planners: neighboring communities and property owners, special interest groups, and the general public. Between 1988 and 1993, over two hundred public meetings were held, with twenty-five thousand attendees, on the Concord Pacific scheme.[20]

Another crucial aspect of this megaproject was the early resolution of the level of provision of community facilities and social housing that would be expected of the developer. The timing of this coincided with the city council's introduction of development cost levies. The planning group working on FCN set out what facilities would be required for this project, area by area. The developer would be expected to convey land for schools, provide space for libraries to lease, and build and convey to the city community centers, day care, and multipurpose rooms. Another notable requirement, unthinkable in most planning environments except perhaps the Netherlands, was that the developer provide sites for 20 percent of residential units as social (that is, publicly subsidized) housing,[21] and that another 25 percent of housing be suitable for families.[22] Lastly, the planners established a benchmark for public parks at a standard of 1.1 hectares (2.75 acres) per thousand people.[23] These provisions were subsequently to become the "Major Project Public Amenity Requirements" imposed on all future megaprojects.

One of the most innovative conceptual emphases in the design guidelines was the ongoing concern with neighborhoods, human scale, and urbanity. As this concern evolved in detailed discussions between planners, architects, and developers, a new architectural form emerged: the tower block with two- and three-story townhouses at street level. The idea of the tower on the lower, townhouse podium was derived from good urban design principles relating to questions such as: how can we maximize the enjoyment of good views by sharing them with as many people as possible? By all means go high, but don't build wide slabs to block too many views and cast big shadows on the people to the north. How do you make sure that there is still a street life, that there are "eyes on the street," that the streets themselves are recognizable spaces, active and safe? The street walls not only provide those functions, they also allow for a variety of land uses (shops and residences) within easy reach of grade. The low-rise podiums provide continuity at street level and help to tie the varying high-rise towers, about four per city block, into a recognizable pattern. However, what is also unique is that the high-rises are grouped around designated, longer-term public view corridors that help maintain the relationship between the high-rise downtown and the mountain backdrop.[24]

Thus does Corbusier meet Jane Jacobs in the new streets of downtown Vancouver. When you walk in this area now, you don't see the blank wall of a monolith. You see a townhouse door, or window, or a shop front. This is high-rise living with a human face, in a dramatic contrast to Corbusian ground-level plans. The streets and the seawall are alive with people walking, jogging, rollerblading, walking their dogs, and walking with their toddlers in strollers. There is a baby boom now in this neighborhood, and a new school has just been built. According to Beasley, Vancouver's chief planner, this tower-townhouse prototype ("the Vancouver model"), developed by brilliant local architects such as Richard Henriquez, Paul Merrick,

False Creek, Vancouver, 1990s. Photograph courtesy of Arni Haraldsson.

and James Cheng, is a Modernist form that provides the mixed-use vibrancy sought by anti-Modernists such as Jacobs, who is now a huge fan of Vancouver's downtown.[25] The key to the success of this new vertical living would appear to be the attention to neighborhood physical, recreational, retail, and social planning. While no post-occupancy evaluations have yet been done, a well-researched article in the *Vancouver Sun* certainly substantiates high enthusiasm for this "antisuburban" lifestyle among residents interviewed.[26]

Beasley has been a persistent believer that you can build human-scale high-density neighborhoods as an alternative to suburbia, and that if you do, buyers will come. Fifteen years after the official development plan for North False Creek was approved, Beasley's vision has proven robust. Vancouver seems to have defeated the "density demon" that has plagued other North American cities, obsessed with the belief that the Good Life is possible only if one owns at least a quarter acre and lives in free-standing, single-family housing. The condominium development model in Vancouver has proven so popular with a new middle class of white-collar professionals that this group is now overrepresented in the inner city and underrepresented in the suburbs, in a reversal of what has happened in most other North American cities.[27] This megaproject has been so successful at each opening of a neighborhood that it is now ten years ahead of schedule (thus "validating" the great length of the early negotiations and public consultations).

The Vancouver Achievement

Most striking about this Vancouver residential megaproject is the triumph of civic over private ambition, or perhaps the successful fusion of the two, since developers certainly have made plenty of money, even though they have contributed significant development cost levies to the city to cover public and social amenities. Perhaps the most transferable and therefore important lesson for other cities in the Vancouver experience is that the development community has learned that certain "quality of life amenities," while costing more to build, result in an upward spiraling of market demand and of local appreciation of such urban environments and that, over time, the bar seems to be irreversibly raised. Creating this climate of social learning for the development community must be attributed to the institutional changes introduced in 1974 and beyond (the new Development Permit Board and Urban Design Advisory Panel) and to the sustained commitment of two remarkable directors of planning.

As a result of this changed climate, Beasley is now able to say, "We have an unusual attitude about development here. Our attitude is 'If you don't measure up, we're not afraid to say *No* in this city.' Many cities are so afraid to say *No* to any developer and so they get what they deserve. But for those other cities it may be above all important to promote a business growth. We want quality of life first."[28] Beasley's vision is that:

> We have an ability to create a city that is to some degree contrary to globalization, contrary to the homogenization of cities going on around the world. It is very unique, and it is very interesting in that it actually competes with those world cities not by trying to be what they are but by being an alternative that they could never be. . . . Because of what we are and where we're sitting in the hierarchy of cities, we have to take advantage of what we have to work with (a spectacular natural setting), to position ourselves to be competitive among cities. . . . This comes down to the quality of life in the city.[29]

Many other factors, most already mentioned, have contributed to Vancouver's special planning environment. Clearly the leadership, the professionalism, and the commitment of the city planning department over three decades has been crucial, but so too has been the support of progressive local politicians. It was an active citizenry from the late 1960s that was and has remained determined to fight for a livable city, that elected these politicians, and that kept them honest. So there has been an important mix of engagement and commitment among citizens, planners, and politicians. Many other North American cities also have active and engaged citizens, but those citizens often seem to repeatedly hit their heads against brick walls. What is different about Vancouver is the receptiveness of the Planning Department to citizens' concerns, and the growing responsiveness of the development community to those concerns.

Other external factors have also been crucial. In the 1970s and 1980s, federal money was available for social housing projects (which enabled the city to fulfill its social mix ideals) and also for the redevelopment of (formerly industrial) Granville Island to include arts and crafts shops, a farmers' market, theater precinct, school of art, community center, and neighborhood park. Granville Island is arguably the most successful yet least internationally known of the many commercial/entertainment/educational waterfront redevelopments, attracting not only local but also regional and international visitors daily.[30]

Institutionally, the devolution of power from province to city in the 1953 Vancouver Charter is another key. So too is the two-tier city-regional planning system in which metropolitan regional goals of growth management, livability, and sustainability have been established through further extensive public consultation processes. But the most essential institutional changes have been the establishment of the Development Permit Board (with its key role for the director of planning) and the Urban Design Advisory Panel, which has created a forum for social learning for urban professionals who are one minute working for private interests and the next advocating public interests.

Another external factor critical to the Vancouver achievement has been its attraction, since the mid-1980s, to Chinese investment and migration. This has created a climate of continuous growth in which it has been possible to extract levies from developers eager to be players. And yet, this change in the city's political and social economy could, as with globalization elsewhere, have undermined the reformist planning vision of the 1970s. Why did this not happen in Vancouver?

Partly because of the cohesiveness and commitment of the local planning and political culture, and partly because of the eagerness of Concord Pacific (through Stanley Kwok, Victor Li, and the Li family) to fit in with this local culture rather than to antagonize it.

Finally, as a planning model, Vancouver's shift to discretionary zoning for the Central Area proved crucial in allowing a flexible approach to development proposals. But this discretionary approach is only as good as the technical competence of planning staff and, even more important, of the values shaping the overall planning environment. Here is perhaps the heart of the Vancouver story: over three decades of public debate and slow gestation processes for official development plans, during which intensive design negotiations were undertaken, a unique local planning and design culture has evolved in which not only public-sector planners but also designers working for private firms have been socialized into a vision for Vancouver of livability and civility, safety and vitality, and have worked collectively to generate the design and planning tools to create such a city.[31]

The creation of this civically oriented design and planning culture is not impossible to replicate. It does not *depend on* a mildly left-wing citizenry any more than it depends on an enlightened development industry or an inspiring and progressive director of planning or mayor. None of these factors is a given or a constant in any city, including Vancouver. All have to be worked at, all the time. But the combination of these factors is critical, and at any one moment in history, at least one of these factors would seem to be necessary to set improvements in motion. So the instructiveness in the Vancouver story is not about "best practices" (a singularly unhelpful approach in my opinion) but rather the idea that any city could embark on this path by daring to take the first step. Whether that first step is taken by a collective civic reform movement, a director of planning, an architect with a different vision of urban life, or even the local newspaper matters less than whether others can be persuaded to make the journey. In short, there are no recipes for building better cities, but we can still learn a lot from inspiring stories.

Notes

Special thanks to Ray Spaxman for numerous conversations about the Vancouver story.

1. Bent Flyvbjerg, Nils Bruzelius, and Werner Rothengatter, *Megaprojects*

and Risk: An Anatomy of Ambition (Cambridge: Cambridge University Press, 2003).

2. Doug Ward, "The Vancouver Miracle," *Vancouver Sun,* September 24, 2004, 1, 6–7; John Punter, *The Vancouver Achievement* (Vancouver: University of British Columbia Press, 2003).

3. Ward, "The Vancouver Miracle," 6.

4. Personal correspondence with Ray Spaxman, November 24, 2004.

5. Punter, *The Vancouver Achievement,* 29.

6. "The DPB, composed of the director of planning and three officials, comes to its decisions at the same meeting where they sit with an Advisory Panel consisting of citizens, design professionals, and development industry representatives, who advise at that meeting after hearing delegations from the applicant and the public. At that meeting they also receive a report from the Urban Design Panel, which consists of architects, landscape architects, and engineers who meet prior to the Board meeting and concentrates on the design aspects of the proposal." Spaxman correspondence.

7. Ibid.

8. Thomas Hutton "Review," *Journal of the American Planning Association* 70, 4 (2004): 485.

9. This was possible in part because there had been an overestimation in the late 1970s of growth in demand for office space, and partly because, since the late 1980s, the value of residential square footage in the Central Area has exceeded that of commercial square footage. In other words, developers saw greater profit opportunities in the residential sector. Personal communication with Michael Gordon, senior planner, Central Area, November 2004.

10. Punter, *The Vancouver Achievement,* 193.

11. Chris Olds, "Globalization and the Production of New Urban Spaces: Pacific Rim Mega-projects in the Late 20th Century," *Environment and Planning A,* 27 (1995): 1713–43.

12. Patrick Malone, *City, Capital, and Water* (London: Routledge, 1996).

13. One reason for this may have been that the price that Concord Pacific paid for the land was regarded as very low by some critics (see Olds, "Globalization and the Production of New Urban Spaces"), thereby already making a significant concession to the developer.

14. Punter, *The Vancouver Achievement,* 223.

15. "Color is an important element in rainy, overcast climates. Vancouver has many bleak days with rain-soaked skies and buildings. In the 1960s the ubiquitous Miesian black bank tower arrived here and quickly convinced Vancouverites that we would do much better with lighter colored buildings, often silhouetted against the near-by mountain backdrop. From all compass points our downtown catches and reflects the sun, creating a beautiful spectacle . . . . So the 'waterfront palette' refers to the requirement for the use of watery/turquoise green glass for all windows, and for light colors for the buildings' main frame." Spaxman correspondence.

16. Punter, *The Vancouver Achievement,* 236.

17. Ibid., 237.

18. Larry Beasley, "The Vancouver Waterfront Experience: The City Perspective," paper presented to Worldwide Waterfront '99 Conference, Vancouver, BC, 2000. See also Larry Beasley, "Vancouver, BC: New Urban Neighborhoods in Old Urban Ways," paper presented to Making Cities Livable Conference, Santa Fe, NM, 1997.

19. "Extremely gifted architects—Richard Henriquez, James Cheng and Roger Hughes—have not only consistently produced buildings that would grace any city, but have [also] helped to develop prototype solutions to the city's design problems that have been adopted by others and enshrined in planning practices. The slim and highly glazed view-articulated tower, the tower and townhouse perimeter block or terrace model, and the low-rise internal street/courtyard for ground-oriented housing were initially nurtured by these architectural practices." Punter, *The Vancouver Achievement,* 382.

20. Ibid., 238.

21. This social housing has been funded by three levels of government, with most funding initially coming from the federal level. However, the federal government stopped funding social housing in 1993, and since then the money has come from the province and the city.

22. City planners had undertaken an extensive study of how to house families at high densities to provide clear criteria. Housing planner and Co-Director of Planning Ann McAfee wrote the study, which provided twelve basic principles for family housing in terms of access to recreation, project size, contextual design, clear definition of private and semiprivate space, privacy, pedestrian routes, active open space, specified play areas, safety and supervision, community identity, unit size, and interior layout. A. McAfee et al., *Housing Families at High Densities* (Planning Department, City of Vancouver, 1978), quoted in Punter, *The Vancouver Achievement,* 95.

23. Punter, *The Vancouver Achievement,* 197.

24. Spaxman correspondence.

25. Ward, "The Vancouver Miracle," 7.

26. Ibid.

27. Ibid.

28. Larry Beasley, quoted in Maged Senbel, "Empathic Leadership in Sustainability Planning" (Ph.D. diss., School of Community and Regional Planning, University of British Columbia, 2005), 58.

29. Ibid., 64.

30. In December 2004, recognition arrived when Granville Island was named "best neighborhood in North America" by the New York–based community development organization Project for Public Spaces. "Granville Island Named Best Neighborhood in North America," *Vancouver Sun,* December 2, 2004, 3.

31. Hutton, "Review," 485.

6

Paved with Good Intentions: Boston's Central Artery Project and a Failure of City Building

Hubert Murray

Nationally notorious, Boston's Big Dig has over the past fifteen years invested $14.5 billion in the new Central Artery Tunnel. Visionary in concept, the underground highway has spawned new development and urban parks that are falling markedly short of their promise. Why?

A generation ago, in the late 1960s and early 1970s, Boston was a place of pilgrimage for anybody interested in cities. Architecturally, the new City Hall and the New England Aquarium were star attractions, and the imaginative refurbishment of Faneuil Hall and Quincy Market showed cities worldwide what could be done with historic fabric. The Boston Redevelopment Authority (BRA) was created in 1957 under Mayor John B. Hynes, then in his third term. Hynes, having beaten the corrupt and charismatic James Michael Curley in 1949, was the first of a succession of reforming mayors. In 1965, under Mayor John F. Collins, BRA Director Monsignor Francis J. Lally unveiled the *1965/1975 General Plan for the City of Boston,* which almost instantly became an icon of city planning and of reformed and progressive city government.[1]

As proposed in the *General Plan,* the aim of the Boston Development Program was "to strengthen those unique assets which have made Boston throughout its history the City of Ideas."[2] In the generation that has passed since those halcyon days of planning, the worm has turned. The BRA, short-staffed and underfunded, is not what it was; planning in the city is once again "a piecemeal approach to a few urgent problems";[3] and the few works of architecture that inspire the new generation of urbanists are in the universities across the river. While Chicago, Portland, and Seattle now lead the country in city planning, Boston has settled into a mode of pragmatic expediency, the "City of Ideas" no more than a historical footnote. While there have been major political and economic shifts in the country as a whole, shifts that have favored free-market opportunism over central planning, Boston has had its own experiences over the past three decades that help explain this change in fortune and attitude. Foremost among these is the Central Artery Tunnel Project, at once the city's most audacious planning initiative in the creation of a transportation infrastructure and apparently its biggest disappointment as urban intervention, for *lack* of planning. Thirty years in gestation from inception to completion, the life of the Artery straddles the generational change in outlook that has taken place in Boston and thus merits special attention.

In the Beginning

The depression of the Central Artery and the Third Harbor Tunnel were proposals contained in the *Boston Transportation Planning Review (BTPR)* of 1972.[4] The *BTPR* was one of the first transportation planning documents in the country to reflect, albeit in diluted form, the groundswell of popular democratic action that two years earlier had brought to a halt the construction of yet another urban highway through the inner city. The plan was in the forefront of the new politics both because of its more democratic planning process—involving "ordinary" citizens and nontechnical participants—and its broader scope, which included evaluation of public transit modes in comparison with highways, as well as the social and environmental factors influencing alternatives. Transportation, economic development, and civic improvement were considered interdependent components in an urban ecosystem.

Tossed about on the seas of local politics for a decade or more, the Central Artery/Third Harbor Tunnel Project got seriously under way in 1982.[5] The Environmental Impact Report (EIR) of 1985/1991 and the Record of Decision in 1991 inherited the genetic makeup of holistic, democratic planning from its parent, the *BTPR*.[6] Permitting documents were developed through an exhaustive process of neighborhood-based popular planning along with an open exposition of technical alternatives. Mitigation measures for land takings and the collateral hardships of construction, which included the monitoring of noise, dust, and air pollution, were supplemented by commitments to expand and improve public transit, subways, and commuter rail and to provide an additional three hundred acres of open space, including public parks in East Boston, Charlestown, and the downtown corridor and extensive additions to the Harborwalk pedestrian path. The rationale for the Third Harbor Tunnel was economic (connecting Logan Airport and South Boston with the hinterland), while the depression of the old I-93 viaduct was promoted not only as an improvement in traffic efficiency but also as an enhancement to the quality of the downtown urban environment. Under the guidance of Fred Salvucci, Governor Michael Dukakis's secretary of transportation, with significant (and sometimes contentious) input from John DeVillars, the secretary of environmental affairs, the EIR was comprehensive, detailed, and democratic, in itself a remarkable monument to planning vision and political will—a worthy, if somewhat unwieldy, child of 1970s thinking.[7]

Slouching toward Banality

At this stage of the story, we must fast forward to the finished product. Ignoring, if we can, the now weeping tunnel walls, we shall concentrate on the city-building aspects of the project and measure its fulfillment of the promise of civic improvement. It is from this perspective that we see inherent weaknesses in the implementation of the plan both as a coordinator of economic development and as a guide for civic enhancement.

The Central Artery project was intended at inception to provide economic stimulus to two major areas of the city: Logan Airport in East Boston and the South Boston waterfront.[8] At the project's completion, both areas have been compromised by agency territorialism and the lack of a coherent vision.

In addition to the Massachusetts Highway Department, which was building the new highway, the three major protagonists other than private developers have been Massport, the largest single landowner on the East and South Boston waterfronts and a self-financing state authority with considerable political autonomy; the Massachusetts Bay Transportation Authority (MBTA), the state agency responsible for public transportation in the Boston metropolitan area, with a board appointed by the governor and dependent on the state for its budget; and the City of Boston, with a relatively powerful mayor under whose jurisdiction fell that land not under the control of state agencies.[9]

Within the terms of the *BTPR* and, more particularly, of the Record of Decision for the Central Artery, the Highway Department was extending I-90 to the airport and the seaport as part of a broader plan for economic revitalization and urban transformation. Underwritten by this massive investment in highway infrastructure, Massport embarked on a $1.5-billion expansion of the airport facilities and a transformation of their seaport property into development parcels. To the extent that this had the makings of a textbook example for urban economic development spurred by public investment, so far so good.

Meanwhile, the MBTA, despite its commitments under the Record of Decision to provide transit connections to these sections of the city, has fallen short on two counts. First, a strategic decision was made to build an autonomous Bus Rapid Transit line (the Silver Line) as a relatively inexpensive alternative to a fully integrated branch of the Red Line, which already extends to the western and southern suburbs. Second, even this more parsimonious model stops short in South Boston (Phase 2), and it is a matter of conjecture as to if and when it will extend to the airport (Phase 3) or make the critical link between South Station and Washington Street that connects back to the South End and Roxbury.[10] The consequences are that the airport remains relatively underserved by public transportation, job opportunities for the neighborhoods are unrealized, and the potential for development of the Boston Seaport is constrained by the limitations of the transit system.

Meanwhile the BRA, which for some years had failed to take an active role in planning this one thousand acres of real estate on the threshold of downtown, was prompted by the opening of the Ted Williams Tunnel in 1995 and the promise of its subsequent (2003) connection to I-90 to produce the *Seaport Public Realm Plan* in 1999.[11] Not only was this plan absent during the planning of the highway in the late 1980s (an absence resulting in an unfortunate siting of major ventilation structures), it also was published after Massport had produced its own plan for the waterfront and was therefore reactive to the development plans of an agency operating under its own mandates.[12] The BRA was in consequence playing catch up to the Artery project, to Massport, to private developers such as the Pritzker family (intent on developing Fan Pier, still in limbo), and even to the state legislature, which in 1998 selected a sixty-acre site in the seaport for the new Boston Convention and Exposition Center without the benefit of a comprehensive transportation plan for this 1.7-million-square-foot facility.[13] What could and should have been a comprehensive economic development plan for the South Boston waterfront, developed in parallel with the plans for the extension of I-90 in the late 1980s, amounted to no more than an urban design plan ten years later, worthy in its goals for streetscape and public space but necessarily reactive to projects already in construction and woefully inadequate in the collection and coordination of solid data serving longer-term principles of urban planning.

For the downtown, however, the weaknesses of city planning are as much aesthetic and programmatic as they are economic. In intention, the rejoining of the city with its waterfront remains close to what was originally planned and to the conditions of the 1991 permitting. Included in the EIR was the vision of the BRA for surface restoration known as the *Boston 2000* plan.[14] In 1988 the BRA, under Stephen Coyle, invited urban design visions for the central corridor from the Spanish architect Ricardo Bofill and local architect

"A Park-like Boulevard," City of Boston, ca. 1992. Courtesy of the Boston Redevelopment Authority.

"The Seamless Web," Boston Society of Architects Central Artery Taskforce, Plan for the Central Artery, ca. 1992. Courtesy of the Boston Redevelopment Authority.

Alex Krieger. The Boston Society of Architects (BSA) invited themselves to the discussion with their own version of the future. Bofill, as one might have predicted, proposed a broad neoclassical boulevard replete with obelisks, amphitheaters, and triumphal arches. The BSA plan proposed a continuum of residential courtyard superblocks on the principle of maintaining a continuous urban fabric and populating the downtown. Krieger took the view that open space would be more successful if framed in a series of public squares, alternating block by block with built form that would generate active and populated sidewalks.[15] The three schemes represented a spectrum of urban theory ranging from the formality of Bofill's grandiose neoclassicism to the pragmatic functionalism of the BSA's urban housing. Krieger's scheme embodied the implied vitality of an urban mixed-use program organized within the formal vocabulary of the urban square. The BRA, in its *Boston 2000* plan, essentially rejected both classical formality and programmatic reality, opting instead for neo-Olmstedian parkland punctuated with cultural pavilions and sidewalk cafés. At this stage there was no indication of how this or any vision might be implemented, either by the state or the city.

It was the BRA's vision, enticingly rendered, that became enshrined in the Record of Decision. Thus, the mandate of 75 percent open space and 25 percent built form became law, reinforced with the city's own zoning legislation that was a detailed textual description of that design.[16] The zoning ordinance mandated, parcel by parcel, specific uses for both open space and buildings, and in the case of buildings, plot coverage, height, floor-area ratio, ground and upper floor uses, and even degrees of transparency.[17]

This degree of prescriptive specificity was unsubstantiated by quantitative data (e.g., demographic projections and land-use inventories), qualitative values (e.g., an analysis of the role of urban open space in relation to the neighborhoods and the region), or a social and political vision that would underwrite this major city renovation. If the purpose of the urban design imagery was to place a foot in the door to reserve space, place, and function for future discussion and development, it had the unfortunate effect of becoming firmly wedged in position as the Massachusetts Turnpike Authority assumed dominant position during the construction period of the project, unwilling and perhaps unable to appreciate the complexities of city building as they encroached upon the prime imperative of getting the highway built.

Despite the passage of time, widespread discussion, and numerous public meetings, the BRA's *Boston 2000* plan, enshrined as it was in the Record of Decision, has remained essentially unchanged, incorporated by the Massachusetts Turnpike Authority into a number of design contracts for the surface restoration above the tunnel and into their 2001 *Master Plan* for the corridor.[18] At all stages of the fifteen-year process, an open public procedure has been adopted in numerous community meetings, true to the letter, if not perhaps to the spirit, of the 1972 article of faith in public participation.

As the process nears its end, and the results of this extended and painstaking process are beginning to be revealed, the outcome can be judged, at best, as respectably banal. If as urban historian Donald Olsen suggests, "Cities . . . can tell us something about the values and aspirations of their rulers, designers, builders, owners, and inhabitants,"[19] we have to ask ourselves whether the Rose Kennedy Greenway does indeed represent Bostonians' highest values and aspirations, and if not, what happened? Reflection on what happened must be three-layered: methodological, conceptual, and political.

Planning to a Design, Not Designing to a Plan

In the methodology of the Central Artery's process, design usurped planning. Notwithstanding Krieger's urban design studies on their behalf, the BRA led with a detailed image of green space punctuated by

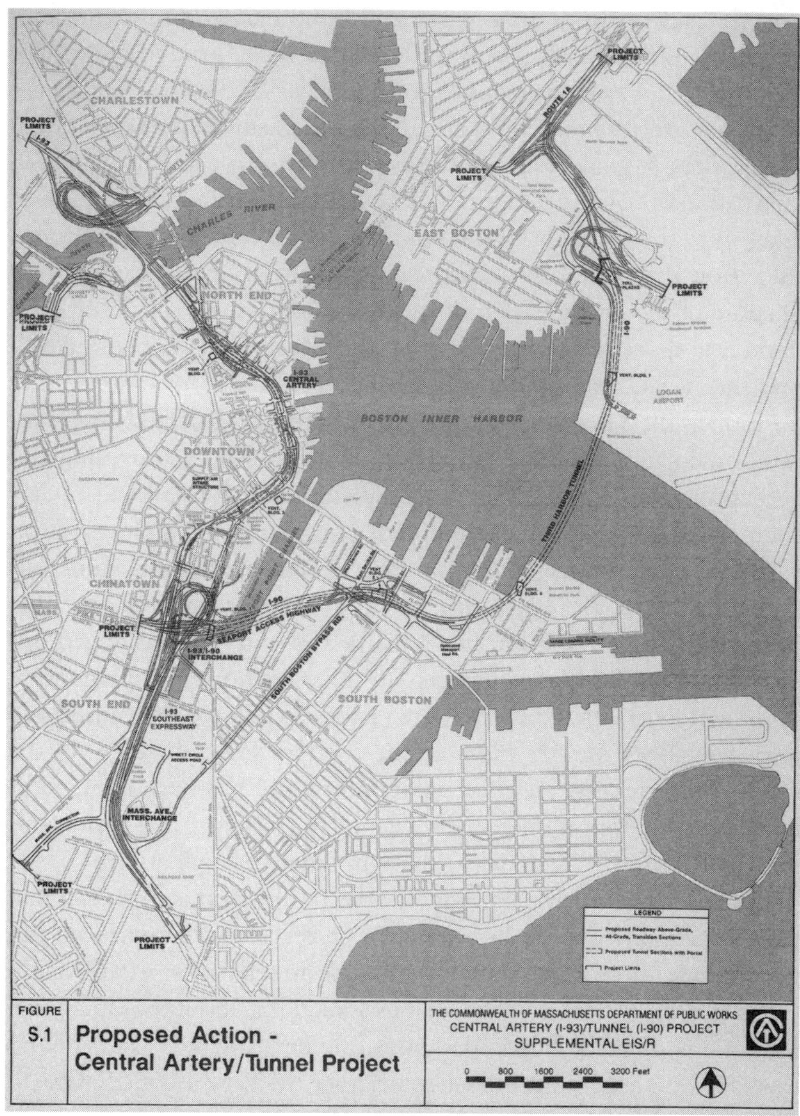

Massachusetts Department of Public Works, Central Artery (I-93)/Tunnel Project, Supplemental EIS/R, Proposed Action, Bechtel/Parsons Brinckerhoff, November 1990. Courtesy of the Massachusetts Department of Public Works.

structures determined by prescriptive zoning but never seriously addressing the planning principles on which the picture was implicitly based. This preemptive rendering of a rosy future by the city's urban designers under Coyle's directive leadership was not only turned back to front in its methodology, it was also developed through a planning process outside the realm of serious discussion, since any modification to the plan would have entailed a lengthy and bureaucratic Notice of Project Change. Granted, there had to be a "vision," and that vision had to be effectively communicated in a public forum. The error was to confuse image with content and to engage the twin imperatives of schedule and cost in defending a plan that was more image than substance, detailed to a degree unwarranted by the data and wrapped in a process that was intended to foreclose further public discourse.

To exacerbate the contradictions of planning to a design rather than designing to a plan, the Massachusetts Turnpike Authority took it upon itself in 2001 to develop a master plan for the central corridor after significant portions of the original design had already been constructed in the form of sidewalks, trees, lighting, and street furniture, thus almost literally casting the urban design image in stone.[20] The planning consultants were under strict injunction not to depart from any of the facts on the ground nor from any designs in preparation. Furthermore, since the Turnpike Authority was directing the master plan, the consultants were limited in their scope to making proposals only within the project boundaries of the highway construction. Thus, adjoining streets and neighborhoods were considered off-limits, rendering the plan itself no more than an isolated object within the broader city fabric.[21] Far from being a master plan, the resulting document was little more than a tightly circumscribed design guideline, again notable for its lack of research or analysis relating to land use or programming. When, finally, landscape architects were appointed to prepare design and construction documents for the parks, they were faced with a street environment already half-built. For the remainder of the Central Artery surface, visual cues were provided by the master plan in the form of renderings, but little hard data gave the projected design a fully reasoned basis.

A Swarm of Small Ideas

Conceptually, the project has suffered from being too much "fox" and too little "hedgehog," with too many small ideas pulling in all directions and too few basic principles leading the way. There has indeed been consistent adherence to the program of public open space. This idea, however, has survived more thanks to the legal body armor of the Record of Decision and subsequently to the focused will of the highway project managers, untutored in urban design and driven by the construction schedule, and rather less to established data, principle, or reason.

While the Boston Society of Architects, the business community, the local media, and other interested parties made proposals over the years to engage the public in a broader discussion on the surface restoration, the Turnpike Authority and its managers successfully curtailed those wider discussions, maintaining progress toward project completion in the face of issues that they regarded as obstacles or distractions in the pursuit of their narrow mission of highway construction. The key issues discussed as part of the ten-year public process focused principally on design and design details and much less on the principles for a broader plan. Sidewalk widths, pedestrian crosswalks, trees species, and curb alignments were the grist of the public planning process, not land use, open space programming, transportation, or even ways to make this new patch of urban space sustainable.[22]

This focus on detail happened for two reasons. First, in public discussion it is easier for nonprofessionals to focus on the concrete issues (planting versus paving, brick versus granite) rather than the abstractions of what makes a city thrive. Second, by confining the discussion to details, the Turnpike Authority (who managed the public meetings) could maintain the project schedule. Thus were the serious issues for public debate not addressed, the boat not rocked, and the project not derailed.

Politically the project has been marked from the beginning as the child of separated parents, the state and the city. The highway project itself has come under the auspices of the Massachusetts Highway Department and later the Massachusetts Turnpike Authority. The main focus of the Central Artery Project has been to construct the highway. The highway is routed, however, through the city, which would, one might assume, give city agencies an equal voice at the table as planning and design progressed. The city, however, sold to the Turnpike Authority the air rights to the highway tunnel, thus relinquishing its rights as owner and placing the Turnpike Authority in control. This has meant that the city's institutional power over the planning and design has not been as strong as it might have been, particularly through the central corridor. By default the highway builders have been the city builders.

Ideally, the task of city building should have been separated from that of highway building. This arrangement would not only have had the advantage of allocating expertise and resources according to professional skill and institutional interest (the BRA and its planners would take care of the city while the Turnpike Authority and its engineers could concentrate on building the highway), it would also have relieved the necessarily extended city planning process from the intense political pressure attendant upon the highway construction.

Compounding this institutional misalignment is the anathema of the project itself, which has caused elected politicians—of all stripes—at city and state levels to avoid the "Big Dig" as much as possible. Unfairly or not, the project was perceived early on as a money sink and a liability, and, even at its best, a public works project that did not have a local neighborhood constituency that would directly translate into votes. For this reason, with isolated exceptions, both the governor and the mayor have sought to keep their distance from what has seemed, especially recently, a black hole. This self-isolation of the political leadership has therefore further undermined city officials in pursuing the cause of city building.[23] Thus, the Turnpike Authority, for (relative) lack of interest, and the city, for (relative) lack of power, have left a void in the planning and urban design process, particularly as it relates to the downtown corridor, which, as we have seen, is not without its inherent complexities.

This political void has been partially filled by substantial efforts from civic associations such as the Artery Business Committee, the Boston Society of Architects, the Boston Greenspace Alliance, and neighborhood-based interest groups. The *Boston Globe* has hosted conferences and published extensively on the remaking of the city, and this has undoubtedly raised the level of public debate. While these civic efforts have had some positive effects on the urban design elements of the greenway, notably the introduction of cultural and recreational buildings into the park corridor, these achievements have been made with great difficulty and over a long time.[24]

As the project enters its final phase and landscape designs are carried into construction, it is hard to avoid the judgment that from one of the biggest and boldest planning moves in the city's history—the radical extension and renovation of the highway infrastructure and the reuniting of the city with its waterfront—a well-mannered if unexciting landscape has emerged, one that will do little to transform the city except insofar as there is no longer an elevated highway separating downtown from the harbor.

Lessons to Be Learned

Of the lessons learned from this lengthy and time-consuming process, some are specific to the Central Artery project and some to Boston itself, while others may have a broader application to U.S. planning and urban design. The following themes emerge.

Divided Responsibilities

The BRA, for all its vaunted powers combining planning and development, is but one of many planning agencies whose decisions affect the city and whose lack of unified leadership under a strong metropolitan authority eviscerates coordinated urban initiatives. It is a great misfortune for Boston that the Turnpike Authority took ownership not only of city land in the Central Artery corridor but also of the city-building project itself, operating outside its sphere of expertise. Similarly, Massport, as the major landowner in the seaport, has seen

Boston Central Artery Corridor, master plan, landscape design framework, lawn area on Parcel 17, 2001. Courtesy of the Massachusetts Turnpike Authority.

fit to develop South Boston in its own autonomous fashion, focusing on port issues, and in advance of the BRA's *Seaport Public Realm Plan*.[25]

Last, the Massachusetts Bay Transit Authority (MBTA), custodian of public transit infrastructure and strapped for cash, has failed to live up to its civic responsibilities in implementing the transit improvements mandated by the Central Artery project. Perhaps more egregious is this agency's failure to proceed with the Urban Ring, a project for circumferential transit that in itself would have a transformative effect on the city's economy and its neighborhoods.[26] In the absence of such coordinated and complementary partnerships and in the absence of political commitment, the BRA and other city development agencies have their hands tied.

The Confusion of Planning and Design

While the highway infrastructure on the Central Artery project itself was meticulously planned, the urban design was not. The permitting of the highway was predicated on traffic projections, connections with other transportation modes, environmental impacts, air quality, and a host of other quantifiable parameters translated into goals and directives. On the other hand, land-use analysis, census and market data, and development principles are remarkably absent in the design proposals propagated by the city. Picturesque representation usurped the planning stage, so that Design became the proxy for Plan. City decoration—acting as a substitute for the planning analysis that necessarily underwrites and directs investment in infrastructure, economic development, and the creation of base conditions for successful urban living—now pervades the profession. Between the quantitative number crunching of the planners and the visionary renderings of the architects, between regional context and site specificity, urban design has to navigate a careful path based on the discipline of solid data infused with social and political vision to give substantial meaning to urban aesthetics. The work of Britain's Urban Task Force and Barcelona's Mayor Pasqual Maragall in transforming planning principles into stunning urban success are leading examples of the intimate connection between political leadership and successful urban design.[27] Those who say that this approach is not transferable to the United States are surrendering before the battle and forgetting the heritage of cities such as Portland, Seattle, Chicago, and indeed Boston in former times.

Whereas the 1965 *General Plan* incorporated data on land use, employment, and infrastructure and was guided by clear goals and principles, the *Boston 2000* plan has no such comprehensive view. This observation is not meant to diminish the importance of the urban design issues posed by the greenway and the creation of meaningful urban space within the void left by the elevated highway. It is to place them in the wider context of the city's development goals. While urban design has grown and provides a much-needed antidote to the formless constructs of traditional planning, the balance may have gone too far in creating forms without content and concepts without analysis. As one of the city's consultants recently put it, the image must market the idea. True, so long as there is an idea to market.

Popular Planning, Political Timidity, and the Erosion of Professional Expertise

A legacy from the *BTPR* and the politics of the 1970s has been adherence to public participation. It is often remarked, with justice, that while "democratic," this process tends to dilute and diffuse quality and direction in design. The acceptance of the principle that whoever shows up at a meeting has an authority equal to anyone else in the room has led to timidity in politicians and designers alike and to an erosion of trust in professional expertise.

While the Central Artery project has over the past ten years consumed hundreds of thousands of hours in public meetings at great expense to the public and to people's time, the effect of this process on design has been to grind it down to a "lowest common denominator," devoid of offensive characteristics. Thus the Wharf District parks designed by EDAW have been relentlessly discussed and criticized in a series of versions unguided by clear program or principle and uninspired by creativity, with the result that in the view of some, they amount to an embodiment of the least offensive checklist of cumulative demands. As with speculative development designed to appeal to the widest market, the overall effect on the urban fabric is characterless homogeneity. Without the commitment of political leaders and without the trust in the technical and aesthetic expertise of design professionals, the process has drifted in a free market of constituency opinion. Paradoxically, the democratization of planning calls for more leadership, not less. Not in the autocratic style of Robert Moses (whose wings would anyway have been institutionally clipped by federal environmental legislation enacted since his time) but more in the persuasive and charismatic style of city mayors such as Norman Rice of Seattle, Joseph Riley of Charleston, or Richard Daley of Chicago, each of whom has had a vision for his city and has led from the front.

Principle or Pragmatism

Principles of urban planning of any kind have been largely ignored in both the work and public discussion about the design of civic space on the Central Artery. Facing the need to complete the highway construction, the Turnpike Authority has often sacrificed principle for expediency as, for example, in the widespread downgrading of paving materials as part of a value engineering exercise, regardless of the commitments to a high-quality public environment. The city would be in a better position to promote and defend the quality of design in the face of such expediency had it been more willing to develop and adhere to principles at the planning stage, principles that might have included stances on programmatic research (the meaning of public space in "walkman" culture), transportation (the future of the private automobile in the city center), environmental policy (attitudes to surface water drainage and retention), the promotion of "front door" activity adjacent to public space, and a host of other items that could have acted as lodestars in the extended and pluralistic decision-making process. The city was not alone. The program for public art, never fully embraced by either the Turnpike Authority or the engineering culture responsible for designing and building the highway, was promptly dropped at the first sign of budgetary difficulties. Proposals for staging international competitions for the design of the central area landscape were effectively smothered at birth under layers of red tape, not to mention the profoundly off-putting complexion of Boston's politics. For all the ballyhoo about this "world-class project," opportunities for young designers as well as for established designers with international reputations have been scarce.[28]

The avoidance of principle or purpose may be attributable at least in part to a cultural mistrust of "theory." It may also be the fear of the city leadership that by adhering too closely to rules, by imposing top down what are often negatively characterized as "conditions," investors will be frightened off and some public constituents enraged. Zoning, it is said in Boston, is where the conversation begins, leaving the field open to lobbying and the contingencies of political pressure. Expediency has become the governing principle of urban planning, and the art of the deal prevails.

The Contrasting Case of Chicago

The 1960s generation of urbanists showed that it was possible to capture the imagination with bold moves (such as the building of the new city hall or, later, the adaptive reuse of Quincy Market) to propel the city onto a new level. While Boston's history of such moves has been episodic, Chicago, at least since Daniel Burnham, has the tradition of city building in its bones. Like Boston, Chicago has invested in its transportation infrastructure. Unlike Boston, Chicago has framed this development in a vision for the city as a whole, notwithstanding its seemingly intractable problem of impoverished neighborhoods. In the past few years, under the leadership of Mayor Richard M. Daley, Chicago has produced a plan for its Central Area, plans for neighborhood open space throughout the city, a sustainability program, and a series of design competitions that enshrine and promote the principles of all this planning activity.[29] Chicago may be one of the few cities in North America that would have no fear in inviting Anish Kapoor to place a 110-foot polished stainless steel blob in the center of its greatest public space. Quickly and relatively inexpensively, the City of Chicago has created Millennium Park, offering the work of great artists, architects, and landscape architects for its citizens' enjoyment, no less.

The lesson from Chicago comes not so much from its architects and planners, engaging as their work may be. It really comes from the boldness of its clients. More than a hundred years ago, Chicago's developers embraced the risk of building tall, installing the world's first elevators, pushing the limits of modern technology in buildings that are now part of the nation's heritage. At home, that same business class reinvented the house, and in so doing created a distinctly American architecture in the Prairie School. Mayor Daley and the city agencies he leads have inherited that tradition of bold thinking.

Urban planning and design achievements do not come without political conviction and steady commitment. It is perhaps not unjust to conclude that the city-building outcome of Boston's vast infrastructure project in its lack of coordination, political stasis, and cultural conservatism does indeed tell us something about the values and aspirations of this city-region. Boston may be excited about the accomplishments of its Red Sox, but if only half of that energy ("Believe!") were translated into civic and political leadership, the city might elevate itself to the level of Fenway Park, becoming once again a destination for urban pilgrimages.

Notes

1. Boston Redevelopment Authority, *1965/1975 General Plan for the City of Boston and the Regional Core* (Boston: March 1965).

2. Ibid., 1.

3. Ibid.

4. A useful summary of the *BTPR* is available on the Web at http:/libraries.mit.edu/rotch/artery/CA_1972.htm. An official overview of this period of highway planning is available on the U.S. Department of Planning Web site in *Urban Transportation Planning in the United States: An Historical Overview: Fifth Edition,* chapter 6. For earlier incarnations of this highway, see also Robert Whitten, *Report on a Thoroughfare Plan for Boston, City Planning Board* (Boston: 1930); Theodore T. McCroskey et al. *Surging Cities* (Boston: Greater Boston Development Committee, 1948).

5. See, for instance, Alan Altshuler and David Luberoff, *Mega-Projects: The Changing Role of Public Investment* (Washington, DC: Brookings Institution, 2003); Thomas P. Hughes, *Rescuing Prometheus* (New York: Pantheon, 1998); Jane Holtz Kay, *Asphalt Nation* (Berkeley: University of California Press, 1997). An excellent account of the planning process is contained in Karl Haglund, *Inventing the Charles River* (Cambridge, MA: MIT Press, 2003).

6. The Final Environmental Impact Report (FEIR) was approved by the Federal Highway Administration in 1985. The Final Supplemental EIR, in twelve volumes, was approved by the state Executive Office of Environmental Affairs and the FHWA in 1991 and is known as the Record of Decision.

7. While the scale and comprehensiveness of the *BTPR* was equal to if not greater than the scope of Boston's *General Plan* of seven years earlier, there was clearly a remarkable change in the politics of planning reflected in the mandated open processes embodied in the *BTPR*.

8. A third development area spawned directly by the Central Artery project

is South Bay, immediately south of Kneeland Street and adjacent to Chinatown's residential district. The BRA's South Bay Planning Study is under way. As with other city planning initiatives occasioned by the Central Artery, the advantage of preemptive or anticipatory planning has not been seized, with the result that the long lead time for development will result in intervening years of blight.

9. For the definition of Plan-A type local governance enshrining a strong mayor with a relatively weak council, see *Massachusetts General Laws: Title VII Cities, Towns and Districts,* chapter 43, section 1: Definitions.

10. This Phase 3 Central Artery commitment, together with an extensive list of other public transit investments that have been left undone, is the subject of intense current political debate. See *Boston Globe,* December 1, 2004, B1.

11. Cooper, Robertson & Partners, *The Seaport Public Realm Plan* (Boston Redevelopment Authority, 1999).

12. Massport, *South Boston Strategic Plan* (April 1999).

13. The Boston Transportation Department published the *Boston Transportation Fact Book and Neighborhood Profiles* in May 2002 and *Boston's Public Transportation and Regional Connections Plan* in March 2003, more than a decade after the Central Artery EIR and three to four years after the South Boston planning efforts referred to in this essay. The lack of a highway connection between the Convention Center and the Back Bay is to be remedied by the Turnpike Authority after considerable lobbying and research undertaken by the business community. The adequacy of the Silver Line to accommodate convention crowds may be less easily resolved.

14. *Boston 2000* (Boston Redevelopment Authority, 1991).

15. Chan, Krieger, Levi Architects Inc., *Urban Design Studies for the Central Artery Corridor* (Boston Redevelopment Authority, 1990).

16. The official documentation failed to clarify what area was the denominator of the 75/25 split, giving rise to various opportunistic interpretations (e.g., building face to building face, curb to curb, with or without the paved highway, etc.). Even the numerator has been in dispute. What has often been claimed to be twenty-seven acres of open space designated for parkland in the corridor is closer to seven acres.

17. City of Boston Zoning Ordinance: Article 49: Central Artery Special District, May 1991.

18. Since 1991 the Central Artery project has been managed and directed by appointees of Republican governors for whom such massive public investment was ideologically problematic. Regardless of individual talent and commitment, therefore, the guiding management principle has been to get the job finished and to avoid when possible any distraction. The clearest example of this approach was the decision by Secretary of Transportation James

Kerasiotes to preemptively override eighteen months of deliberation by the Bridge Design Review Committee, which was evaluating alternative means of crossing the Charles River at North Station. SMWM/The Cecil Group with The Halvorson Company, *Boston Central Artery Corridor Master Plan* (Massachusetts Turnpike Authority, 2001).

19. Donald J. Olsen, *The City as a Work of Art* (New Haven: Yale University Press, 1986), ix.

20. *Boston Central Artery Corridor Master Plan.*

21. This particular matter is being addressed, albeit a little late, by the BRA's "Crossroads Initiative" of 2004, which explores opportunities for rejoining and upgrading those streets previously severed by the elevated highway.

22. In the absence of a program for the proposed open space coming from the Turnpike Authority or the city, the Artery Business Committee commissioned Sasaki Associates to produce one for the Wharf District. The ABC/Sasaki *Program and Design Guidelines for the Wharf District Parks* (September 2003) was incorporated into the EDAW design for that section of the Greenway. Worthy as this private effort has been, it remains unfortunately symptomatic that this programming exercise was not undertaken by the city prior to their development of the *Boston 2000* plan.

23. The recent tunnel leaks serve to illustrate this syndrome. The real damage incurred by these widely publicized construction faults is not the leaks themselves (which can be fixed) but the loss of faith in public investment, a far weightier political issue.

24. In a series of studies encompassing planning, urban design, financing, and governance, the Artery Business Committee and its consultants have undertaken research and developed new programming and design approaches to the development and management of the Central Artery corridor. This work has resulted in a series of planning and urban design proposals for Chinatown, the Wharf District, and the Bulfinch Triangle, a public open space and recreation program for the Wharf District, and a model for the financing and management of the park system when it is finished.

25. Cooper, Robertson et al., *The Seaport Public Realm Plan.*

26. U.S. Department of Transportation, *Environmental Impact Statement on the Urban Ring Project Phase 2,* 2001.

27. See *Towards an Urban Renaissance: Final Report of the Urban Task Force* (London: Department of the Environment, Transportation and the Regions, 1999).

28. Much to her credit, Kathryn Gustafson has been an exception to the rule in overcoming these vicissitudes. Her design for the North End Parks has more or less survived the public process under the guidance and protection of her local partners, Crosby Schlessinger and Smallridge of Boston. Private

initiatives have so far attracted proposals from nonprofit organizations with designs by Daniel Libeskind and Moshe Safdie.

29. For example, among a host of city planning and environmental initiatives are *Chicago Central Area Plan, 2002*; *CitySpace Plan, 1998*; *Chicago River Plan, 1998*; and the *Ford Calumet Environmental Center Competition, 2003*.

7

Public Planning and Private Initiative: The South Boston Waterfront

Matthew J. Kiefer

Public places have in recent decades been increasingly created by private developers through exactions imposed by government bodies. This strange brew of profit motive and public benefit is fraught with complications. Not only may such public amenities be inadequately designed, built, and maintained to truly serve the public, but their imposition may also hinder development that would be good for civic life. This essay explores these complexities and proposes steps to address current problems through a close look at a major development site in Boston.

As responsibility for conceiving and constructing public streets, sidewalks, sewers, and parks—the armature of American cities—continues to shift from government to private actors who enter the land-use regulatory arena, planning and creation of the public realm are becoming more a *result* of private initiative than a *driver* of it. The important and only dimly recognized implications of this shift are explored here in the context of the long-sought-for development of the "Fan Pier" site on Boston's next development frontier, the South Boston waterfront.

The Fan Pier saga illustrates how the confluence of several forces—the shifting role of public planning commensurate with shrinking federal aid to cities, strained municipal budgets, and public distrust of large-scale planning initiatives, along with a more rigorous approval

Pei Cobb Freed and Partners, John Joseph Moakley United States Courthouse and Harborpark, Boston, Massachusetts, 1998. Photograph copyright 1998 Steve Rosenthal.

process and a strong development climate—has changed the planning landscape. Starved of resources for implementation of planning ideas, city government has found ways to harness private market forces to produce public benefits that reduced municipal budgets can no longer fund. The development approval process has become a kind of surrogate for planning—or perhaps even planning itself in a new guise—the crucible in which cities are actually formed, one piece at a time, largely by private initiative.[1] This changed landscape has consequences for each of the actors in the land-use drama: city government, private developers, and the public.

South Boston Waterfront

Located across a narrow shipping channel from downtown, the South Boston waterfront district comprises a thousand acres of filled land created by private companies under licenses from the Commonwealth of Massachusetts beginning in the 1870s—privatization is not as recent as is commonly supposed. By extending the landmass of the South

Boston peninsula into tidal flats in Boston Harbor, this land-making allowed for the expansion of industrial and commercial enterprises and the shipping and railroad facilities necessary to accommodate them.[2] With these original functions now mostly gone, the area is controlled by a handful of large public and private landowners. While two major public buildings have opened—a federal courthouse and a convention center—and some large-scale private development has also occurred, much of the land is vacant or lightly used.

During Boston's 1980s real estate boom, the area was anointed as the place where the downtown core was most likely to expand. This was based on the beliefs (which have proved only partially true) that the city's economy would continue to grow and that buildable sites in the downtown core would be insufficient to meet this demand. Large public investments have been directed to this area to stimulate its development. As part of Boston's $14-billion Central Artery/Tunnel project, the area has received on- and off-ramps connecting to Logan Airport, the Massachusetts Turnpike, and I-93 North and South. A $600-million bus rapid transit line known as the Silver Line—the first new transit line in the system in a century, linking the area to a major intermodal transit hub at South Station and to Logan Airport—is now operational.[3] The court-mandated cleanup of Boston Harbor has also increased the amenity value of waterfront sites.

Fan Pier

The most prominent development site in the area is the so-called Fan Pier parcel, twenty-one acres on the waterfront just across the shipping channel, named for the shape of the railroad sidings it once contained and now used for surface parking for downtown commuters. Following a lengthy approval process for an office-oriented project in the 1980s—a project that faltered when the city's real estate market stalled—and following ensuing litigation, a company controlled by the Pritzker family, owners of the Hyatt hotels, became owners of the site. After early attempts to sell the site to developers, in early 1999 the Pritzker family hired a development manager to obtain public approvals for its own ambitious new development plan.[4]

Several things happened in the decade between the abandonment of the first Fan Pier proposal and the creation of the second. First, the regulatory landscape became more complex.[5] In 1990, the Commonwealth of Massachusetts adopted much stricter regulations governing development of filled former tidelands such as the Fan Pier for non-water-dependent uses. (In fact, the Fan Pier would become the first major test of this new regulatory scheme, as discussed below.) The City of Boston adopted zoning-based large-project approval requirements: a comprehensive transportation, urban design, and environmental impact review and a "linkage" program requiring proponents of large-scale commercial and institutional facilities to pay into city-controlled funds for affordable housing and job creation.[6]

Instigated by the 1980s real estate boom, these stricter regulatory schemes landed with a resounding thud as large-scale private development virtually ceased in Boston during the early 1990s. This pause gave time for more progressive planning ideas to take root in city policy, emphasizing mixed use, pedestrian orientation, and a more legible street and block pattern. These were reflected in the city's *Seaport Public Realm Plan* for the district, prepared by Cooper, Robertson & Partners and released in 1999. This plan identified locations for infrastructure needs ranging from truck routes to local streets to parks and marinas, and suggested general building heights, densities, and mixes of uses.[7] Its strong emphasis on residential uses challenged the prevailing assumption that the medium- to high-density downtown core, dominated by commercial, government, institutional, and cultural uses, would merely spread across the channel. This housing emphasis had two purposes: it would create a more activity-filled district, and it would help address the city's growing housing shortage, a major priority of Boston Mayor Thomas M. Menino. The mayor's housing emphasis was further reflected in an executive order issued in 2000, which established an inclusionary housing policy that now requires any new housing development of more than ten units that seeks discretionary city approval to make 13 percent of its units affordable to low- and moderate-income households.[8]

Over several years of public review, engaging the vigorous participation of waterfront advocates and others, the Fan Pier's development team navigated these new (or newly strengthened) regulatory processes to obtain approvals for a $1.2-billion, three-million-square-foot mixed-use project. In contrast to the 1980s proposal, widely criticized as a suburban-style office park, the second Fan Pier project included almost as much residential space (approximately 1.1 million square feet) as office space (approximately 1.2 million square feet); a 650-room hotel; approximately 135,000 square feet of ground-floor retail, restaurant, and other active uses; and a 2,285-space underground parking garage.

The approved proposal parsed the superblock into nine city-sized blocks and obligated the developer not only to create this network of essentially public streets, sidewalks, and utilities but also to excavate a six-acre cove and provide a recreational marina and boat dock, a public walkway along the water, significant public parks, and over 100,000 square feet of civic, cultural, and public amenities, including a prime waterfront site for a museum of contemporary art—ironically, the only element of the plan actually under way at this writing.[9] The cost of these public commitments has been pegged at $70 million, slightly over 5 percent of the total project cost and more than half of the site's intended price.[10]

The significant public benefits that this profit-motivated development project was required to provide have played a role in the site's current development impasse. During summer and fall of 2004, the owners put the development site on the market, and two successive would-be purchasers declined to proceed after examining the project's feasibility and expressing concern about the cost of complying with public entitlements. City officials announced their intention to hold the first buyer's feet to the fire on public commitments, and the developer repeatedly pledged to honor them—until it let its purchase agreement lapse. By the time the second bidder emerged, the city indicated some willingness to consider altering the cost and timing of public commitments, garnering criticism from some quarters for compromising too easily.[11] When the second development team backed out, the lead developer cited the cost of these commitments as a major challenge to development feasibility,[12] although it could be argued that the site's acquisition price should have been adjusted downward to account for these costs.

The Perils of Private Creation of the Public Realm

Although the Fan Pier site has benefited perhaps more than most from public investment in the regional infrastructure of highway, transit, and harbor improvements, it is not unusual in being asked to create its own local infrastructure of streets, walkways, sewers, and parks and to provide significant public benefits and amenities as the price of approval. In fact, it is important to acknowledge the advantages of privatizing the creation of public amenities. It reduces the burden on city planning staff and financial resources. Like other forms of outsourcing, it shifts the burden to lower-cost producers—in this case, to private parties, unencumbered by civil service, competitive bidding, and other progressive reforms. By forcing private parties to forge consensus through the project approval process, it also reduces the political capital that public officials must spend for development. And in general, taxpayers are only too happy to have private developers fund public improvements.

This reliance on private initiative can in theory increase the chance of implementation of projects that benefit the public. As the pace of social and technological change accelerates and as capital becomes more mobile and real estate markets more volatile, it is increasingly difficult for long lead-time planning efforts to keep up. Profit-motivated developers are more nimble and can be counted on to anticipate market realities more accurately than the public sector. Lastly, the amenities undoubtedly have some value to the developers who build them by improving the marketability of their projects, although they generally view this somewhat intangible value to be far outweighed by the very real up-front cost.

But here as elsewhere, there is no such thing as a free lunch. Such microscale planning cannot hope to address the broader consequences of growth. More subtly, reliance on private initiative leveraged through development exactions further undermines government's prestige, increasing the public's perception that only the private sector can build things efficiently, thus justifying further efforts to reduce government resources for direct action and to shift responsibility to private actors through the regulatory process. Activists often view these exactions as an abdication of government's responsibility that distorts regulatory decision making as the city becomes too dependent on private development, allowing the fox to guard the hen house.[13]

Harvard Graduate School of Design Professor Jerold Kayden has addressed the consequences in illuminating empirical detail in the context of the 1961 incentive zoning ordinance in New York City, where forty years of experience demonstrates that private actors have little incentive to plan, build, and maintain public accommodations in ways most useful to the public.[14] As a consequence, their efforts require a degree of public sector standard setting, monitoring, and enforcement that they do not always receive.

The cost of these public benefits also induces developers to reduce project costs in other areas—such as architectural distinction—and to seek larger projects capable of supporting the cost of public benefits, thus encouraging more public opposition. Because developers are creating pieces of the public realm, they arouse a greater number of stakeholders who, quite understandably, care passionately about the design of streets, parks, and other public amenities—especially parks, whose privatization engenders particular anguish for its tendency toward commercialization and subtle exclusion.

The current approach also requires the public sector to calibrate exactions and incentives to achieve the maximum level of public benefits that profit-motivated developers are willing to provide. This itself creates several challenges. City government must meter development rights so as to allow projects of sufficient scale to fund public benefits, but not so large that they create unacceptable impacts or increase public opposition. These mixed motivations further fuel the distrust of anti-development activists, as well as developers, who fear that government will lower the as-of-right baseline in order to exact more public benefits. Since the public can only guess at how much burden the developer's pro forma can bear, it tends to push private projects to the edge of feasibility before declaring that the developer has done enough—often a lengthy and rancorous process. The very length of this process, in the face of increasingly volatile real estate markets, means that once a project has received the public entitlements necessary to proceed, the market that it intended to capture may have evaporated. This mismatch between approval and market cycles may then require a recalibration of benefits—as may occur in the future with the Fan Pier—further delaying implementation.

Finally, this reliance on private initiative means that public realm creation is erratic and opportunistic in timing and location. After two decades, the prime Fan Pier site is still a windswept expanse of asphalt that the public rarely visits—only the parked cars of suburban commuters enjoy the splendid harbor views. The public walkway along the water's edge, one segment of a continuous forty-three-mile-long public Harborwalk first envisioned more than fifteen years ago, will not be built and active until development proceeds. Public realm creation occurs in locations where development occurs, not where the public need is greatest, its timing driven by market cycles, not by planning imperatives.

Responses

A possible response to these problems is to recast the role of government. As Oliver Wendell Holmes observed, taxes are the price of civilization, and it is tempting to speculate about what might change voters' appetite to pay a higher proportion of that price. The result would be a world of beguiling clarity in which activist government, however imperfectly, is the creator and steward of the public realm, free to make straightforward, predictable decisions regarding private development. Private actors, freed from these cumbersome responsibilities, would willingly abide by the more predictable rules and build more modestly scaled projects more expeditiously. But before we become too captivated by this vision, it is useful to remember that the last era of muscular government, during the 1950s and 1960s, the era of public housing, urban renewal, and highway building, had unfortunate consequences from which we have not yet fully recovered.

In any case, private initiative in fulfilling planning goals has a long history, and, like it or not, municipal resources for implementation are unlikely to increase in the near future. Crises, from climate change to severe traffic congestion,[15] could alter this over time, but meanwhile the trend is toward more privatization, not less, so it seems sensible to focus on addressing the challenges presented by current conditions. Mostly, this means working to establish clear ground rules for these new roles and responsibilities to produce more predictable outcomes.

So, for instance, the City of Boston could build on its generally high-quality district concept plans, such as the *Seaport Public Realm Plan,* to adopt more detailed citywide design, performance, and maintenance standards for privately created infrastructure. This would involve public review, ideally involving both developers and advocates, who would both stand to benefit from the exercise. The standards would, one hopes, accommodate or even encourage variations by neighborhood to reflect local character and to allow for the idiosyncrasy that characterizes so much of Boston's existing built fabric.

The city could also establish expenditure guidelines for public benefits expected of private actors, perhaps calibrated by project size and use, the for-profit or nonprofit nature of the project proponent, and the degree of public need for each area of the city. Informed by a planning effort to identify infrastructure needs by area, the city could direct the public benefits generated by an individual project to areas where the need is greatest. In this way, high-value areas generating more dense development could subsidize more low-value areas with greater need.

Of course, such programs would need to be carefully crafted to comport with limits on exactions imposed by the U.S. Supreme Court and would need to overcome political pressures from affected neighborhoods to keep such benefits close to home.[16] But initiatives along these lines would regularize the approval process for individual projects and reduce case-by-case public negotiation of the design and amount of public benefits, which requires stakeholders to reinvent the world with every project.[17] This more predictable development process would reduce obstacles to the creation of the public realm and would create a level of consistency that would help allay public concerns about opportunism.

Even with this improvement, the new privatized planning paradigm would not be perfect, but at least until voters are willing to increase government's mandate to address planning needs directly, it may have to do. Had this clear set of expectations been in place from the start, the Fan Pier project and the $70-million worth of public improvements it will leverage might well be in place today.

Notes

1. In fact, the Boston Redevelopment Authority has exacted so many promises from private developers that it has recently hired a former IRS attorney as a full-time compliance officer—a "promise keeper." Thomas Keane Jr., "BRA Forgets Need to Enforce the Law," *Boston Herald,* October 20, 2004, editorial section.

2. Nancy S. Seasholes, *Gaining Ground: A History of Landmaking in Boston* (Cambridge, MA: MIT Press, 2003), 287–333.

3. Anthony Flint, "S. Boston Split on Route Shift for Silver Line," *Boston Globe,* December 17, 2004, B1.

4. Anthony Flint, "Fan Pier Plans Fan Out: New Proposal Mixes Public Access, Housing, Business," *Boston Globe,* March 10, 1999, B1.

5. It seems curious that land-use regulation has become more rigorous in the era of limited government. It is perhaps more accurate to observe that land-use regulation, which is conducted mostly at the local level (particularly with diminishing federal involvement), has become more rigorous in some cities, particularly those with a strong development climate, a distinct physical character, and an engaged citizenry, like Boston and San Francisco.

6. For information about the environmental impact review requirement,

see Large Project Review, City of Boston Zoning Code, Article 80B. See also Development Impact Project Review, City of Boston Zoning Code, Article 80A.

7. Cooper, Robertson & Partners, *The Seaport Public Realm Plan* (Boston Redevelopment Authority, 1999).

8. Mayor's Executive Order Relative to Affordable Housing, February 29, 2000, as amended.

9. Final Project Impact Report/Final Environmental Impact Report for the Fan Pier Project, July 31, 2001 (EOEA No. 12083).

10. Scott van Voorhis, "Mall King Hints Fan Pier Plan Overloaded, Impossible," *Boston Herald,* November 10, 2004, business section.

11. Thomas C. Palmer, "Karp Team Won't Buy Fan Pier: For the Second Time in Two Months, A Deal for Site Fails," *Boston Globe,* November 9, 2004, D1.

12. Van Voorhis, "Mall King Hints Fan Pier Plan Overloaded."

13. Shirley Kressel, "Keep the Public in Public Space," *Boston Globe,* May 19, 2001, D7.

14. Jerold Kayden, *Privately Owned Public Space* (New York: John Wiley & Sons, 2000).

15. In a recent survey, Massachusetts residents ranked traffic congestion as the second highest quality-of-life issue in need of major improvement, trailing only affordable housing. "The Pursuit of Happiness: A Survey in the Quality of Life in Massachusetts," Massachusetts Institute for a New Commonwealth (MassINC) cited in "Mass. Commuting," a joint project of MassINC and the University of Massachusetts Donahue Institute, October 2004, 4.

16. See *Dolan v. City of Tigard,* 512 U.S. 374 (1994); *Nollan v. California Coastal Commission,* 483 U.S. 825 (1977).

17. Like the general increase in litigation, could this be part of a larger trend toward relying on formal legal processes to resolve disputes in the face of diminishing social consensus?

8

Omaha by Design—All of It: New Prospects in Urban Planning and Design

Jonathan Barnett

Over breakfast in Omaha, we were talking about design guidelines. The architect for a proposed Wal-Mart had been asked at a public hearing why his building looked so much less appealing than a Wal-Mart in Fort Collins. His reply struck a nerve: "Fort Collins has design guidelines, and you don't." Omaha's political and business leaders had been committed for years to improving downtown. Now they became aware that the image of the city could be shaped by decisions on prominent sites along peripheral highways. But then they decided that Omaha needed design guidelines, not just for big-box stores but for *the whole city.*

How do you write design guidelines for a whole city? One part of such a system of guidelines would have to engage the community's beliefs—the design values on which everyone could agree. Finding agreement would be similar to creating guidelines for a historic district, when you must define the essence of what needs to be preserved, except that the range of values would be much larger and more varied. Devising guidelines for a Wal-Mart or other suburban retail structure in a parking lot, surrounded by other retail buildings in their parking lots, is not like the more familiar task of writing guidelines for closely spaced buildings on downtown streets. Fort Collins does indeed have regulations for the massing and facades of big retail buildings, but the problem is also their placement, how they relate to the street, to the topography, and to other buildings and uses. The subdivisions and strip malls going up on the outskirts of Omaha were another significant design issue. Was there any hope of shaping them through development regulation in ways that could be compared to the "regulating plan" at Kentlands or other planned communities where design follows agreements between the developer and the lot buyer?

This, then, is a case study of an unusually ambitious yet feasible plan.

Omaha's Design Character

When I first came to Omaha, I was struck by how hilly it is, not at all like my expectation for a city on the Great Plains. The early settlers would have found a rolling landscape with meandering creeks along the valleys. Most of the tall trees would have been on or near the creek banks. As they came over the hills, the settlers would have seen a green valley framed by the hills beyond. Today the creeks are in culverts or have been straightened and channeled until they look like little more than drainage-ways. The city's street grid was laid out with no concern for topography. The underlying landscape is almost forgotten. Natives of Omaha are startled when I tell them they live in a city of hills.

Old photographs of downtown Omaha show it looking much like other traditional U.S. downtowns, except that the streets are steeper than most. Six- and eight-story buildings line the sidewalks, with shops on the ground floor and tenants' advertising signs on the second- and even third-floor windows and walls. The Old Market district preserves some of this original character, but downtown today is much more open, redeveloped at the scale of the automobile, not the pedestrian. Omaha has a new skyline of tall buildings, a courthouse by Pei Cobb Freed and Partners, an addition to the Joslyn Art Museum by Norman Foster, and, under construction, a performing arts center by the Polshek Partnership. A few historic buildings survive, and some presentable new ones, plus the usual ration of parking lots and nondescript service structures. The old meat-packing district is gone, replaced by parks. The Gene Leahy Mall, designed by Lawrence Halprin in the 1970s, is a multiblock park with a sunken artificial river. At the end of the park are fountains that appear to direct water under a street and down to the surprisingly big lake in the adjacent Heartland of America Park at the edge of the Missouri River. Along the lake is the landscaped campus of Con-Agra, one of five Fortune 500 companies with headquarters in Omaha.

Downtown today is only one business center in a chain that stretches westward along Dodge Street twenty miles to the current city limits. This long east-west corridor, plus five or six north-south business streets that intersect it, is the real downtown for this city of four hundred thousand within a metropolitan area of eight hundred thousand. The developments along these streets form Omaha's front door, the places used by the most people, where having design guidelines is most important.

The older parts of Omaha have traditional neighborhoods with tree-lined streets and local schools, churches, and shops. Many of these neighborhoods are strong and attractive; others show signs of social stress. Much city investment has gone into preserving and improving the poorest neighborhoods; you don't see scenes of inner-city devastation. In the rapidly developing newer parts of Omaha, houses and apartments are built in tracts sorted out by selling price or rental category, with few if any trees or other neighborhood amenities. Shopping is in strip centers. Schools and institutions each have big separate sites. If you want a newly built house, you are unlikely to find one in a traditional neighborhood.

The Design Process

I proposed that we divide the design guidelines for Omaha into three subsets—Green, Civic, and Neighborhood—which correspond to three potential constituencies for urban design—environmentalists, civic or cultural organizations, and neighborhood activists. Relating development to the city's characteristic geomorphology, designing desirable and recognizable places, and creating an appropriate setting for community life are also basic issues within the Green, Civic, and Neighborhood categories.

I made it a principle that my colleagues and I from Wallace Roberts and Todd would not propose anything in Omaha that had not been implemented successfully somewhere. What would be special in Omaha would be applying urban design comprehensively to a whole city. We also decided to work within the framework of Omaha's

1997 master plan. This permitted us to concentrate on design and not unlock all the interrelated variables about such issues as infrastructure, health services, and education. All the master plan components have design implications, but revisiting every recently made decision would have stopped us before we got started.

I outlined a yearlong process for studying alternatives, arriving at agreed-on design concepts, and devising means of implementation. A group of leading businesses and foundations funded the process through the Omaha Community Foundation. The mayor became an enthusiastic supporter, contributing the participation of the planning department and other city agencies. The planning director and a former chancellor of the University of Nebraska at Omaha cochaired a working review committee that included neighborhood representatives, real estate developers, design and engineering professionals, business executives, union leaders, and government officials—a group representing all the categories of people who would have to agree if the city were to adopt major changes in the way it manages development.

We realized that if we opened the review committee meetings to the press and the public, the committee members would be less likely to speak frankly. Our solution was to have a public meeting later in the day, when we would make the same presentation, often improved by comments made at the earlier review. Some committee members attended the public meetings so they could hear and report on what was said. The *Omaha World Herald* and the TV channels covered the public meetings, and the *World Herald* ran articles about the Green, Civic, and Neighborhood issues beforehand, which helped produce a large turnout, never less than several hundred people.

I asked an old friend and colleague, Brian Blaesser, to advise us. Brian, a partner at Robinson and Cole, a firm well known for its expertise in land-use law, is the author of books and articles on design guidelines and development regulation.[1] He played a reassuring role as someone who knew what cities really could do and have done to promote and regulate development. His participation gave credibility to our design proposals and kept us firmly in the realm of the possible.

Connie Spellman, the director of a program called Lively Omaha, managed our yearlong effort for the Community Foundation. She worked with the city to create the review committee, arranged for speakers to carry the message to community and business groups, and went to many meetings herself with the funders backing the project, and with business and political leaders, to make progress reports and explain the urban design process. Her staff managed the logistics of the review committee and public meetings and organized and distributed all the public information. She changed the name of the process from "the Omaha comprehensive urban design plan" to Omaha by Design.

Green Omaha

Ian McHarg wrote vividly of the need to design with, not against, natural forces.[2] Anne Spirn added the observation that the city continues to exist within nature, no matter how ignorant the decision makers may be about ecology.[3] Our Green campaign started with Omaha's hills and the creeks that run along the valleys. Many of these creeks now run at the bottom of deep channels, and what you see from the trails that run along them are the backs of buildings, dumpsters, and service entrances. The buildings along the creeks make it impossible to restore the meandering streams and wetlands. But the waters of Brush Creek in Kansas City had been raised by breakaway dams as part of the Country Club Plaza Plan that I helped frame in the late 1980s. The result is a stream that looks like a river, rather than a trickle at the bottom of a concrete culvert. Here was a successfully implemented design that could be a model for Omaha. Our slides of Brush Creek and our drawings showing Omaha's creek waters raised and the banks landscaped helped convince people that creek frontages could be assets.

Omaha is subject to sudden heavy rainstorms and flash floods. Public safety issues should keep development out of the floodplains along the creeks. We showed how flood-protection policies in Tulsa, which has a similar weather pattern and ecology, have had the effect of creating a citywide open-space system along the creeks there. So our proposal was to combine necessary flood protection with the landscaped creeks to form a park system that adds value to the whole city, especially to the properties outside the floodplain but facing the creek.

New federal water-quality standards and flood protection both require retention of stormwater on the hillsides flanking the creeks. We showed examples and made drawings of "green" parking lots, a direction suggested by a participant in one of our community meetings, to show how water retention could be achieved by landscaping within the lots, saving land area for the developer. Another benefit: the heat-island effect could be greatly reduced by tree cover in large parking lots. Comparable concepts have been implemented in other communities by modifying requirements for parking and water retention already in subdivision ordinances.

Omaha's turn-of-the-last-century park and boulevard plan created scenic drives along the ridgelines and a legacy of green streets in the older parts of Omaha. The eighteen hundred acres of sparsely planted land on the fringes of Omaha's limited-access highways could also be opportunities for large-scale landscape design. We showed highway landscaping in California and in cities like Charlotte and Chicago, and made drawings to demonstrate how trees, native grasses, and flowering plants could make big changes in the experience of the highway at costs within the means of corporate sponsors or private donors.

The city already has programs for planting and replacing street trees, but the subdivision ordinance has not required developers to plant trees on new residential streets. Since tree planting requirements are routine in subdivision ordinances, we suggested adding them in Omaha. We also delineated a network of "framework streets," where tree planting and landscaping would be most important.

These proposals will lead to a connected system of tree-lined streets, parks, waterways, and landscapes that will become the setting for Omaha's neighborhoods and business centers.

Rapid urbanization of the city's surrounding farmland is the other obvious Green issue. The city has already reserved future suburban park sites in the master plan, since its planning jurisdiction extends three miles from its current borders. The master plan also designates areas where population densities should be kept low to preserve environmentally sensitive areas. We would have liked to have proposed growth boundaries. The population of Omaha is growing at the rate of 1 percent a year, but land is urbanizing much faster than would be required by population increases alone, as is true almost everywhere in the United States. Growth boundaries had been considered for the master plan but not included, since Nebraska law does not support the kinds of growth boundaries that, at least until the 2004 election, had been in force in Oregon. We approached this part of the Green agenda indirectly. Policies proposed under the Civic heading will result in greater residential and office densities within already developed parts of Omaha. Attracting some development away from the edges can slow down the rate at which farms give way to urbanization.

Civic Omaha

We asked the working committee to help us list the most memorable places within the city, the places that received the most use, and the gathering places for public events. The results confirmed our observation that Omaha's Dodge Street is like Atlanta's Peachtree Street or Los Angeles's Wilshire Boulevard, linking a series of important locations that extend westward from the original downtown for twenty miles. Most of the other important places are along major north-south streets that connect to Dodge.

It would be confusing to call all these areas downtown, so we called them "areas of civic importance," but together they function as the downtown of the metropolitan city Omaha has become. We proposed that these areas of civic importance be mapped in the zoning ordinance as an overlay district. The areas within the overlay will be subject to the kinds of design guidelines for building placement, pedestrian access, and concealing service areas used in successful downtowns elsewhere. Urban designers have had extensive experience in managing downtown development and can point to many successful outcomes.

One lesson: government investment in streets and other public spaces is just as important as the standards placed on private development. New commitments for planting street trees, providing high-quality streetlights, and rationalizing traffic and parking information signs are proposed within the areas of civic importance. The design guidelines for private investment will be principally about the relationship of buildings to streets, just as they are in traditional downtowns, but allowing for the differences in scale.

It will take a long time to bring all the areas designated as civically important up to a downtown standard. In addition to legislation and public investment, it will require the creation of business improvement districts to mobilize the resources of the stakeholders within each subarea. Just as owners have not thought of their land along Omaha's creeks as waterfront property, the property owners

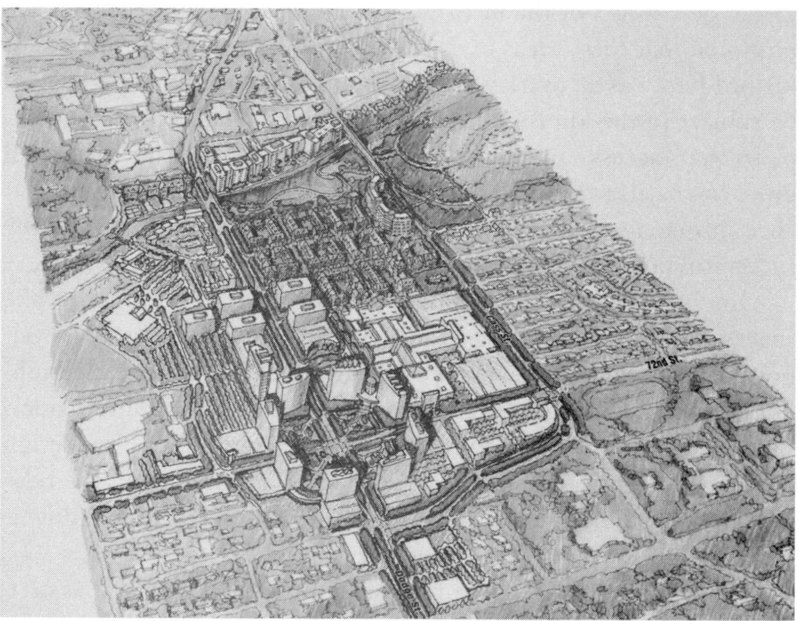

Wallace Roberts & Todd's proposal to transform Omaha's Crossroads area into a "Civic Place District" shows the area today *(top)* and its future build-out *(bottom).* There is a new lake where the two creeks meet, and a new public square at the intersection of Dodge and Seventy-second Streets. Courtesy of Jonathan Barnett/Wallace Roberts & Todd.

in these areas of civic importance have not thought of themselves as having the opportunities and responsibilities that go with being in a downtown.

We made designs for six Civic Place Districts within the areas of civic importance—two in the traditional downtown and four at strategic locations along the Dodge Street corridor. There will be more, but these offer prototypes. Each is designed around one or more public places, and the design guidelines, which use build-to and set-back lines to place building frontages around the public space and suggest locations for towers and parking garages, are based on the increased value that proximity to such a space can create. The feasibility of the guideline comes from the public investment, plus a substantial increase in permitted development under zoning. These are locations that have the potential to become urban places, with a mix of apartments and offices as well as retail, and that can help draw people back from increasingly remote suburban districts. Specific plans like these can create opportunities for developments not possible today because no individual property owner is in a position to organize them.

We also proposed set-back/build-to lines for buildings along major commercial corridors outside the areas of civic importance, plus minimum landscaping requirements for each development, and requirements for confining aboveground utilities to one side of the street, preferably in an easement behind the buildings.

Under Nebraska law, property owners can create a Sanitary and Improvement District in nonurban areas before they are annexed to a city. These "SIDS" can make capital improvements, supported by tax assessments within the district. When the district is annexed, the city takes over the debt obligation. Omaha can set standards for Sanitary and Improvement Districts that are ultimately expected to be annexed by saying what will be acceptable and what will not. Omaha's master plan already sets requirements for different sizes of commercial centers, from 10 to 160 acres, which will be acceptable when they are annexed to the city.

We saw that this power allowed Omaha to ask for mixed-use, walkable centers instead of strip malls. We took a typical real-estate industry model, "the life-style retail center," where stores and restaurants are organized along a street and not just facing a parking lot, and proposed adding apartments and offices to produce places friendly to pedestrians. We prepared design guidelines for these pedestrian-oriented, mixed-use centers to replace the categories of commercial centers already in the master plan. The guidelines show street and sidewalk configurations and building placements for each category of center.

These designs set up a framework that allows development to become more intense as time goes on, without rebuilding the initial structures. Such places can reach a high enough population density and include enough destinations to enable them to be served by rapid transit, which in turn will reinforce compact, walkable patterns of development and draw businesses and residents that might otherwise go even farther out. We made drawings to show how this transformation could take place at key locations.

Other civic design proposals set standards for illuminating significant buildings and other structures, like highway bridges, and call for more funding for public art and for the establishment of a design review board to control the quality of publicly financed projects.

Neighborhood Omaha

Omaha has hundreds of areas considered neighborhoods; more than seventy neighborhood associations maintain Web sites and issue newsletters. There are too many of these organizations for the city to respond to each effectively. A recent planning study had helped create an alliance of neighborhoods in Omaha's midtown area, where leaders got to know each other by participating in the planning process. We proposed that the city draw boundaries that would create fourteen Neighborhood Alliance Districts, not unlike Washington's Advisory Neighborhood Commission Districts and New York City's Community Planning Districts. The mayor immediately saw the value in doing this and made it his policy before we had even finished our plan.

We proposed that each of these Neighborhood Alliance areas should receive help from the city in developing its own plan, which would include taking the Green and Civic principles established citywide and applying them at a smaller scale. The Neighborhood Alliance plans should also deal with preserving and enhancing retail in older neighborhoods and adding neighborhood retail and other amenities in post-1950 neighborhoods. We provided illustrations showing how such plans could be done. We also illustrated how to create walkable neighborhoods with their own retail and civic centers as the city expands. New traditional neighborhoods are sometimes created as part of individual developments; we show how neighborhoods where people can walk to some destinations could become common.

Implementation

Brian Blaesser advised us from the beginning that we had to be very clear about what we wanted to accomplish before we got into extended discussions about how to do it. The planning director suggested that the first step toward implementation should be the adoption of our work as the official Urban Design Element of the Master Plan, something actually called for in Omaha's charter. Such an element had never been prepared and was not included when the city adopted its latest master plan. Our final report became the draft Urban Design Master Plan Element, along with a framework report by Blaesser, setting forth the legal basis for future implementation measures.

Altogether, the twenty-one Green, Civic, and Neighborhood goals, objectives, and policies require seventy-three implementation proposals, including administrative changes by the city, legislative changes, capital projects, and opportunities for privately funded initiatives. The last of the public meetings in the Omaha by Design process endorsed these proposals.

The *Omaha World Herald* printed a sixteen-page insert for the Sunday newspaper that gave a much bigger audience an opportunity to examine the urban design goals and rank them from high priority (1) to lowest priority (5), either by sending back a form that was part of the insert or by answering the same questions on the Omaha by Design Web site. More than thirteen hundred responses have been received. Since the survey is available on the Web, a few responses have come in from outside the city, including one from Vancouver and several from Texas. All twenty-one goals received strong support; very few people checked 4 or 5; the score for most goals averaged in the high 1s or low 2s.

The objectives receiving the most support are those that produce the most benefit for the most people: green streets, the park system along the creeks, high quality of public buildings, conservation of older buildings, preservation of older neighborhoods, and creating neighborhoods in new areas. The Civic Place Districts and other goals requiring guidelines for building design scored well but not as well. Public art, the lighting of landmarks, "green" parking lots, and highway beautification, which might be considered the most obvious urban design measures, were lower priorities.

The Urban Design Element has now been approved unanimously by both the planning commission and the city council. The city has announced three pilot projects that are going forward right away. An engineering study is looking at how to raise the creek waters and create a landscaped lake in the key Crossroads district. Landscape architect Michael Van Valkenburgh has been retained to prepare the first of the Civic Place Districts within and around the Gene Leahy Mall downtown. This plan will find ways to enhance the multiblock park originally designed by Lawrence Halprin to make it more accessible and usable, and will look at ways of connecting the Old Market district, where most of the downtown restaurants are, to the new Performing Arts Center, which is on the opposite side of the mall. The mayor has announced the first of the Neighborhood Alliance studies in the Benson area, which will include its traditional retail district as well as surrounding residential neighborhoods, most developed just after World War II.

Still to come: the actual legislation for the design guidelines, administrative changes that will enable the city to manage oversight of urban design, and a program of design-oriented capital improvements that can be financed publicly or privately.

Pie in the Sky?

"This plan is not pie in the sky." Del Weber, the cochair of the review committee, said this at most of the early public meetings, no doubt responding to skeptical comments he had been hearing. Weber, formerly the chancellor of the University of Nebraska at Omaha and a former president of the Omaha Community Foundation, would not give this assurance if he didn't believe, from his long experience of civic life in Omaha, that the proposals in the plan are feasible. Everything in the plan has been done successfully somewhere; each proposal is based on a clear scenario about how it can be implemented. Making the planning report into the Urban Design Element of the Omaha Master Plan, adopted by the planning commission and city council, avoids having the document gathering dust on the shelf so often mentioned as the destination for most plans. It is now city policy.

How much of Omaha by Design is actually implemented will depend on how effectively we have framed its proposals to create new value for property owners and the public. While some results should be visible within five years, it is not a plan that can be carried to completion right away but a campaign that can take a generation or more to bring to fruition. When the work is done, new parks will have been created around the creek systems throughout the city; the main highways and streets across the city will be landscaped; stores, offices, and apartments will be grouped around identifiable civic locations that have the presence of traditional downtowns; and each cluster of neighborhoods will have its own amenities and centers of civic life.

Omaha's leadership understands the economic importance of keeping Omaha competitive by making it a place where people choose to live and work in a time when people can choose to live and work almost anywhere. The leadership and the public now see how urban design and planning can help improve their city.

Notes

1. Brian William Blaesser is author of *Discretionary Land Use Controls: Avoiding Invitations to Abuse of Discretion* (St. Paul, MN: West Group, 1997); and *Condemnation of Property: Practice and Strategies for Winning Just Compensation* (New York: Wiley Law Publications, 1994); he is coeditor, with Alan C. Weinstein, of *Land Use and the Constitution* (Chicago: Planners Press, 1989).

2. See especially Ian McHarg, *Design with Nature* (1969; New York: J. Wiley, 1992).

3. See Anne Spirn, *The Granite Garden: Urban Nature and Human Design* (New York: Basic Books, 1984).

9

Is Eminent Domain for Economic Development Constitutional?

Jerold S. Kayden

Urban planners employ a carefully guarded arsenal of treasured techniques to implement their planning ideas. The most well-known mechanism is zoning, through which publicly prepared ideas for land use and built form are imposed on private property owners whether they like it or not. Another longstanding implementation technique is eminent domain, the power of government to take private property against the will of the owner, as long as the taking is for a public use and just compensation is paid. Both zoning and eminent domain infringe on an individual's private property interest, yet courts routinely sided with urban planners for much of the twentieth century when asked to review whether such techniques violated constitutional protections for private property.[1]

Since the late 1980s, however, judges have started to take a closer look at the application of zoning and related regulatory techniques. Could planning conditions attached to development approval be too intrusive?[2] More recently, that closer look widened to eminent domain. Could taking private property for privately managed urban redevelopment be improper?[3] With a zest for the dramatic, the Supreme Court of the United States accepted two cases for review this term that hold the potential for determining just how hard a look judges will take in eminent domain and zoning contexts. In *Kelo v. City of New*

London,[4] the Court will consider when or whether government may take land, including single-family homes, by eminent domain and turn the properties over to private developers to advance economic development purposes. In *Lingle v. Chevron USA*,[5] a case dealing with facts that have little relation to land-use planning, the Court will nonetheless consider whether the Constitution requires a stronger planning rationale for zoning and other regulatory actions than most planners had thought. Taken together, the cases could enervate elements of the implementation arsenal and expand the role of judges in land-use planning. This article addresses the eminent domain piece of the arsenal.

For centuries governments have wielded the power of eminent domain to take private property for public use, as long as fair market value is paid to the owner. *Eminent* means standing above others, *domain* means complete and absolute ownership, and government thus stands above owners and takes ownership of their property. The phrase *eminent domain* does not appear as such in the U.S. Constitution, but the power is endorsed by negative implication in the Fifth Amendment's Just Compensation Clause, which declares, "nor shall private property be taken for public use, without just compensation." That clause effectively serves two masters: individuals who are protected against government seizure of their land for nonpublic or public uses unaccompanied by adequate compensation, and the government now authorized to take private property for public use.

Legal challenges to the exercise of eminent domain commonly present two issues: first, is the exercise of eminent domain legislatively authorized? second, is it constitutional? Typical American federal, state, and local legislation authorizes "condition precedent" and "condition subsequent" takings.[6] A condition precedent taking occurs when government exercises the power to redress a before-the-taking existing use of land. The most notorious condition precedent has been that before it may be taken, land must be "blighted," the legislative mantra of the federal urban renewal program. Condition subsequent takings occur when land is expropriated to create a future, after-the-taking traditionally public use such as a highway, reservoir, airport runway, rail right-of-way, or public facility. Takings for highways do not typically require a finding of blight, even if a review of the historical record would empirically and sadly suggest that highways could only be routed through poor areas qualifying as legislatively "blighted."

The central constitutional question, "what is a public use?" was seemingly resolved fifty years ago in the U.S. Supreme Court's *Berman v. Parker* case.[7] Berman, owner of a department store, was a bit player in a typical urban renewal play. The District of Columbia Redevelopment Land Agency was authorized by legislation to acquire land by eminent domain for the redevelopment of blighted territory. Although Berman's store itself was not blighted, he had the misfortune of being surrounded by blight, and the Redevelopment Land Agency took his store along with everything else around him for redevelopment into middle-class housing and other uses.

In a unanimous decision penned in majestic prose by Justice William O. Douglas, the Court upheld this exercise of the eminent domain power, stating, "The concept of the public welfare is broad and inclusive[]. The values it represents are spiritual as well as physical, aesthetic as well as monetary. It is within the power of the legislature to determine that the community should be beautiful as well as healthy, spacious as well as clean, well-balanced as well as carefully patrolled."[8] Once the legislature has spoken, intoned Justice Douglas, "the public interest has been declared in terms well-nigh conclusive."[9]

And not only that, but "[o]nce the object is within the authority of [the legislature], the means by which it will be attained is also for [the legislature] to determine."[10] Those means could include use of private parties for accomplishing the condition subsequent use: "the public end may be as well or better served through an agency of private enterprise than through a department of government. . . . We cannot say that public ownership is the sole method of promoting the public purposes of community redevelopment projects."[11] In short, a transfer from one private party—in this case Mr. Berman—to another private party for the purpose of developing middle-class housing, with the government as intermediary, was not constitutionally barred.

Thirty years later, in the 1984 *Hawaii Housing Authority v. Midkiff* case,[12] the Court expressly reaffirmed the deferential standard of constitutional review it had initially announced in *Berman*. The Hawaii legislature had enacted a law authorizing the taking of land from the owners of large estates in order to give the land to individuals currently leasing small pieces of the estates. The purpose of the law was to remedy market failure caused by land oligopolies; the reality of the law was a government-orchestrated redistribution of land from rich private owners to poor private owners. Without a blink, the Court unanimously upheld the legislation, asserting, "When the legislature's purpose is legitimate and its means are not irrational, our cases make clear that empirical debates over the wisdom of takings—no less than debates over the wisdom of other kinds of socioeconomic legislation—are not to be carried out in the federal courts."[13]

At least until recently, when asked, state courts have similarly deferred to government exercise of the eminent domain power. The signature case was the 1981 *Poletown Neighborhood Council v. City of Detroit* opinion.[14] General Motors proposed to build a new automobile plant in Detroit, wanted to locate it in place of a residential neighborhood known as Poletown, and asked the city to take the land from the neighborhood owners. Then-Mayor Coleman Young could hardly have been thrilled with his Hobson's choice: give in to GM, keep jobs and tax revenue in Detroit, and destroy a neighborhood, or save the neighborhood and lose the factory to, say, Alabama. He chose the former. Under authority granted by state law to take land for industrial and commercial purposes, a local economic development agency seized the land, homes were demolished, people were displaced, and GM constructed its assembly plant.

The Michigan Supreme Court succinctly framed the issue: the "heart of this dispute is whether the proposed condemnation is for the primary benefit of the public or the private user."[15] The court announced that the power of eminent domain may not be exercised "without substantial proof that the public is primarily to be benefited," and where power is exercised "in a way that benefits specific and identifiable private interests, a court inspects with heightened scrutiny the claim that the public interest is the predominant interest being advanced. Such public benefit cannot be speculative or marginal but must be clear and significant."[16] Here, the court found, the power of eminent domain was used primarily to accomplish the essential public purposes of alleviating unemployment and revitalizing the economic base of the community, while the benefit to the private interest was merely incidental. The taking stood its ground.

By the mid-1980s, it would have been hard to identify many constitutional land-use scholars who thought there was much of a constitutional limit to what urban planners could accomplish through eminent domain. Yes, the city could not take private property and turn it over to the mayor's brother-in-law to benefit the family. But eminent domain for economic development was acceptable as long as economic development was the real purpose. Whatever limitations would be placed on this power arose from policy revulsion over past practices—the familiar accounts of neighborhoods being sacrificed in favor of questionable superblock developments[17]—rather than any constitutional boundary.

Recently, however, that legal certainty has become less certain. Several state court cases have undercut unfettered exercise of eminent domain power,[18] most surprisingly perhaps in *County of Wayne v. Hathcock,*[19] an opinion announced by the Michigan Supreme Court that expressly disavows its earlier *Poletown* ruling. Wayne County adopted a $2-billion airport construction program for a new terminal and runway. The Federal Aviation Administration provided $21 million to the county to assist in purchasing the land of neighboring homeowners as part of a noise abatement strategy. The county ultimately acquired more land to develop a business and technology park, known as the Pinnacle Project, consisting of a conference center, hotel accommodations, and a recreational facility. The project assertedly would create thirty thousand jobs and $350 million in tax revenue. Property owners of nineteen parcels needed for the project refused to accept the county's buyout offer and challenged the land taking in court.

This time out, the Michigan Supreme Court declared the proposed takings unconstitutional under the Michigan state constitution. Transfers from one private entity to another are constitutional, said the court, but only where there is a public necessity like railroads and canals that need a straight line, where the private entity remains accountable to the public through ongoing oversight, or where the land itself presents a condition precedent like blight. *Poletown,* declared the court, "is most notable for its radical and unabashed departure from the entirety of this Court's pre-1963 eminent domain jurisprudence."[20] The opinion raised the ante with an ultimate hypothetical: "[I]f one's ownership of private property is forever subject to the government's determination that another private party would put one's land to better use, then the ownership of real property is perpetually threatened by the expansion plans of any large discount retailer, 'megastore,' or the like."[21] In other words, Wal-Mart could displace *your* single-family home as long as it could persuade a local government to lend its eminent domain power.

Michigan is one thing, the law of the land another. That is about to change. The U.S. Supreme Court's upcoming decision in *Kelo v. City of New London*[22] could convert the *County of Wayne v. Hathcock* rule into a national imperative. A New London, Connecticut, public development corporation had prepared a development plan for a ninety-acre site along the Thames River, adjacent to a newly constructed global research facility for the Pfizer pharmaceutical company and a state park. As with all economic development schemes, the purpose of the plan was to create jobs and increase tax and other revenue, as well as to encourage public access to the waterfront and generally kick-start revitalization. To implement the plan, the corporation would condemn some land parcels and, while retaining ownership, lease them to a private developer for ninety-nine years at $1 per year. The developer would build high-tech research office space, parking, and a marina, producing 518 to 867 construction jobs, 718 to 1,362 direct jobs, 500 to 940 indirect jobs, and $680,544 to $1,249,843 in property taxes. The precision of the numbers is almost laughable unless one is familiar with the ability of economic development consultants to generate statistics. Ms. Kelo, a single-family homeowner on-site, and several other homeowners declined to make their land available for the project.

After disposing of a statutory claim, the Connecticut Supreme Court tackled the constitutional issue under both federal and state constitutions and upheld the land takings, as generally authorized by state legislation and as applied in this case. It declined a parsing of the phrase *public use* that would produce a meaning different than public purpose, citing an 1866 Connecticut case rejecting the argument that *public use* should be strictly construed to "mean [] possession, occupation, direct enjoyment, by the public."[23] Even in the mid-1800s, said the court, the dictionary definition was broader: *use* can mean utility or something productive of benefit.

As to the general idea of eminent domain for economic development, the court concluded that "economic development plans that the appropriate legislative authority rationally has determined will promote municipal economic development by creating new jobs, increasing tax and other revenues, and otherwise revitalizing distressed urban areas, constitute a valid public use for the exercise of the eminent domain power under either the state or federal constitutions."[24] On the other hand, cautioned the justices, "an exercise of the eminent domain power would be an unreasonable violation of the public use clause if the facts and circumstances of the particular case reveal that the taking was primarily intended to benefit a private party, rather than primarily to benefit the public,"[25] thereby echoing the overruled heightened scrutiny *Poletown* rule. Here, the public benefit was primary: it was good that a major corporation like Pfizer is moving into a down-on-its-luck city like New London, there is no indication that the city wanted to help Pfizer and its shareholders for their own sakes, and jobs and taxes are at stake. In Connecticut, unlike Michigan, eminent domain for economic development is constitutional.

How will the U.S. Supreme Court analyze the case? Does the plain language of *public use* supply the answer, disqualifying condition subsequent uses developed and controlled by private interests? In a world in which the line between public and private is increasingly blurred, a plain language textual analysis hardly advances the inquiry. Ownership or control cannot be the key indicia in an era of privatization in which private parties can construct, own, and operate just about anything that government previously owned and operated.[26] Even a historical analysis of what the framers meant by *public use* would similarly suffer from a context of mixed public-private roles and responsibilities. A highway today may be operated by private parties charging tolls.[27] And, in any event, who's to say that a hotel lobby isn't used by the public, at least in the sense of a plain language interpretation of *public use*?

Does the purpose of the just compensation clause, to assure that "some people alone [do not] bear public burdens which, in all fairness and justice, should be borne by the public as a whole,"[28] shed light? In general, compensation has been viewed as the sole and adequate palliative for individuals saddled with public burdens, but does money really pay for everything? Clearly the individuals in this and similar cases are saying "No," since they are not willing to sell at fair-market value, and maybe not at any price. Are not these individuals in the end asserting a different interest in private property, one less easily monetized because only the specific sellers and not prospective buyers have a property interest defined by ties to *that* local community, history, memory, and personal identity?[29] Of course, such ties can be equally undone by classic public-use takings, for example, for a highway, but perhaps there is an extra "demoralization" cost suffered by condemnees when their land is given over to a private party developing uses less obviously public.[30]

What about the effect of judicial precedents and the rule of stare decisis? Blunt overrules do occur, but rarely.[31] Instead, the Court could attempt heroically to distinguish its previous precedents to limit or invalidate eminent domain for economic development. The Court could read *Berman* and *Midkiff* as condition precedent cases—*Berman* had blight, *Midkiff* had land oligopoly—whereas Wayne County and New London just had single-family homeowners minding their own business, but that fact was never a point of emphasis in the previous decisions. To be sure, takings for economic development projects have historically lived in the twilight of condition precedent/condition subsequent categories. Most have been combinations, in that the land taken was "blighted" and was subsequently redeveloped by private interests for housing, hotels, retail centers, and office buildings. Recent examples, however, have included takings of land not "blighted" in any commonsense fashion, but nonetheless disappointing in the eyes of local government in terms of job and tax generation. It is hard to see how the "public use" proviso allows government to take land in order to convert it from blighted to unblighted conditions, but stops government from taking land it wishes to convert from good- to better- (at least in government eyes) performing conditions.

Alternatively, will the Court bless eminent domain for economic development but revoke its previously deferential standard of review and substitute a tougher scrutiny that demands proof that public purpose will stand a good chance of being accomplished? Such rules may help keep local governments "real" and "studious" in their planning efforts, but it is never hard to find economic development experts to document the 251.82 jobs that will be created. And would a higher-level scrutiny then extend to reviews of all socioeconomic legislation enacted and administered by government under "police" and "tax-and-spend" powers regulating or granting public subsidies to private development in service of economic development ends?[32]

Where does this leave urban planning? It is important to draw a distinction between the *constitutionality* and the *wisdom* of using eminent domain for economic development. The judicial role is limited. Does the "public use" proviso of the just compensation clause prevent government from taking unblighted land from one private owner and giving it to another private owner for economic development purposes? In a world in which city officials spend much of their days figuring out how to leverage local resources to create or maintain jobs, enhance the built environment, and strengthen the tax base, all under the banner of economic development, it would be anomalous to invalidate one urban development strategy while granting other regulatory and public subsidy approaches free rein. It may be unfortunate that local governments feel forced to compete with each other for jobs and tax revenues, but that is not properly fixable by a tough-love interpretation of public use.

Even if the Court endorses the view that eminent domain can be used for economic development, with the caveat that the economic development purpose be palpable and demonstrable, urban planners are hardly off the hook. With decades of urban renewal history to recall, viewing single-family neighborhoods as fields of dreams for job- and tax-generating uses may require corrective lenses. Granting legislatures and administrators, rather than courts, the practical authority to decide when somebody's home may be forcibly seized only tees up the question of whether and when government should exercise this awesome power. Preserving what there is of community and fundamental fairness to individual property owners are not outside the decision-making calculus of urban planners. The Constitution is not the only preventive against planning mistakes.

A Postscript

On June 23, 2005, the U.S. Supreme Court announced its decision in *Kelo,* ruling five-to-four that the City of New London's exercise of the power of eminent domain did not violate the "public use" provision of the just compensation clause. In an opinion written by Justice Stevens, joined by Justices Kennedy, Souter, Ginsburg, and Breyer, the Court noted how it had repeatedly rejected over many years a literal, narrow interpretation of the phrase *public use* requiring the taken property to be put into use by the general public. Indeed, the Court repeatedly cited *Berman v. Parker* and *Hawaii Housing Authority v. Midkiff* for this and other conclusions. Instead, said the Court, the question is whether the city's development plan serves a public purpose. The majority concluded that promoting economic development is a traditional and long-accepted function of government. Moreover, noted the Court, the city has through careful deliberation formulated a comprehensive plan for the area, one whose goals include, but are not limited to, new jobs and increased tax revenues. The mere fact that the private sector is employed to help achieve these goals does not invalidate that effort. In sum, the Court candidly declined to assume a significant oversight role in reviewing government exercise of its eminent domain power for economic development.

In her dissenting opinion, Justice O'Connor, joined by Chief Justice Rehnquist, Justice Scalia, and Justice Thomas, wrote that the majority's decision rendered all private property vulnerable to government land takings whose purpose is to upgrade from a lesser to a better use. In a memorable turn of phrase, Justice O'Connor opined that "[n]othing is to prevent the State from replacing any Motel 6 with a Ritz-Carlton, any home with a shopping mall, or any farm with a factory." Justice Kennedy wrote a separate opinion concurring with the majority, while Justice Thomas wrote a separate dissenting opinion.

Notes

1. See Jerold S. Kayden, "Charting the Constitutional Court of Private Property: Learning from the 20th Century," in *Private Property in the 21st Century: The Future of an American Ideal,* ed. Harvey M. Jacobs (Northampton, MA: Edward Elgar, 2004).

2. See *Dolan v. City of Tigard,* 512 U.S. 374 (1994); *Nollan v. California Coastal Commission,* 483 U.S. 825 (1987).

3. See, for example, *Southwestern Illinois Development Authority v. National City Environmental,* 768 N.E.2d 1 (Ill. 2002), *cert. denied,* 537 U.S. 880 (2002).

4. No. 04-108, cert. granted, 9/28/04.

5. No. 04-163, cert. granted, 10/12/04.

6. These phrases are the author's invention and are not in common use.

7. 348 U.S. 26 (1954).

8. Id. at 33.

9. Id. at 32.

10. Id. at 33.

11. Id. at 33, 34.

12. 467 U.S. 229 (1984).

13. Id. at 242, 243.

14. 410 Mich. 616, 304 N.W.2d 455 (1981).

15. Id. at 458.

16. Id. at 459, 460.

17. See, for example, Mindy Thompson Fullilove, *Root Shock: How Tearing Up City Neighborhoods Hurts America, and What We Can Do About It* (New York: Ballantine, 2004); Herbert J. Gans, *The Urban Villagers* (New York: Free Press of Glencoe, 1962); Jane Jacobs, *The Death and Life of Great American Cities* (New York: Random House, 1961).

18. See, for example, *Southwestern Illinois Development Authority v.*

National City Environmental, 768 N.E.2d 1 (Ill. 2002), cert denied, 537 U.S. 880 (2002).

19. 684 N.W.2d 765 (Mich. 2004); 2004 Mich. LEXIS 1693.

20. Id. LEXIS at 53.

21. Id. LEXIS at 58.

22. 268 Conn. 1, 843 A.2d 500, *cert. granted,* No. 04-108, 9/28/04.

23. Id. at 31.

24. Id. at 46.

25. Id. at 62, 63.

26. See Jerold S. Kayden, The New York City Department of City Planning, The Municipal Art Society of New York, *Privately Owned Public Space: The New York City Experience* (New York: John Wiley & Sons, 2000) (public space privatization).

27. Dan Mihalopoulos, "Council May Skip on Way to Bank; Analysts Whistle over Skyway Deal," *Chicago Tribune,* October 27, 2004, C 1 (ninety-nine-year lease to private company to operate Chicago Skyway).

28. See *Armstrong v. United States,* 364 U.S. 40, 49 (1960).

29. See Margaret Radin, *The Liberal Conception of Property: Cross Currents in the Jurisprudence of Takings,* 88 Colum. L. Rev. 1667, 1689-91 (1988).

30. See Frank Michelman, *Property, Utility, and Fairness: Comments on the Ethical Foundations of Just Compensation Law,* 80 Harv. L. Rev. 1165, 1210-11 (1967).

31. See, for example, *Brown v. Board of Education,* 347 U.S. 483 (1954), overruling *Plessy v. Ferguson,* 163 U.S. 537 (1896).

32. See *Lingle v. Chevron USA,* No. 04-163, *cert. granted,* 10/12/04.

10 From New Regionalism to the Urban Network: Changing the Paradigm of Growth

Peter Calthorpe

For many Americans, the everyday environment of freeways, subdivisions, malls, and office parks is a given—an inescapable reality that covertly structures their time, associations, and opportunities. This landscape is so familiar that it is practically unseen and often goes unquestioned. But when questioned, it is framed as the inevitable consequence of market forces and cultural desires—a destiny in which public policy plays merely a supporting role. For many, it is an unassailable expression of the American Dream.

But this landscape is the product not just of free market forces but also of a distinct planning paradigm supported by highly coordinated policies. The planning paradigm is a collage of low-density, single-use areas connected by a road network dedicated to the car: sprawl. The policies that support this paradigm are many and sometimes obscure: state and federal road standards and funding that favor autos over transit or pedestrians, secondary market financing and mortgage tax deductions that bias our housing types, a fiscal structure in suburban towns and counties that directs land use away from denser housing to tax-rich commercial development, and a set of underwriting standards in most banks that leaves no place for mixed-use developments. All this adds up to a self-reinforcing system of public policies and institutional bias that is tenacious and entrenched.

This system delivers a standardized product, one that varies little across the country. It survives not by conspiracy or even ideology, but by the ossification of old habits. As conditions shift with new demographics, new technologies, and new environmental challenges, this old pattern inhibits innovation and much needed change.

But cracks are appearing. Traffic congestion, lack of affordable housing, environmental pollution, loss of open space, and fractured communities are now standard in most metropolitan areas. Like its segregated land uses, sprawl's problems are treated in isolation by specialists with single-purpose policies; the big picture is out of focus. Our assumptions about the inevitability of this land-use pattern are so powerful that we think the solutions to these problems are just more of the same: more highways to cure congestion, more subdivisions to provide affordable housing, and lower-density development to stave off pollution, crime, and loss of community.

Sprawl's roots are thought to be an organic expression of our culture, but much in our culture has changed, and the old paradigm has not kept up. New planning models are emerging—alternatives that can satisfy market needs with less environmental impact, less cost, less congestion, and perhaps stronger communities.

These new models must be conceived at both regional and local levels in large-scale strategic planning connected to a new sense of urban design. They will involve new codes, technical standards, policies, financing mechanisms, and land-use patterns. Guiding these shifts in policy, standards, and local planning will be the emerging practice of regional design.

A region is unconsciously "designed" by its highway structure, road standards, finance systems, tax structure, environmental regulations, and zoning types. Local planning is largely at the mercy of these forces. Towns are reduced to determining the quantity of development more than its type or overall impact. Smaller jurisdictions and counties can downzone residential, overzone tax-producing commercial, and shift troublesome uses to other parts of the region, but do little more. They do not and mainly cannot overhaul the type of development that can be financed, the nature of the infrastructure that passes through their area, or the economic context that defines their range of land-use choices. All of that is in the domain of regional design, state programs, and federal policy.

Regional planning and innovative forms of urbanism are the keys to opening up new directions in development. And they must happen simultaneously. A progressive regional plan without new forms of local development will be an empty set of goals, while local land-use change without regional coordination will be haphazard. Luckily we have several good examples of this interdependent process and important emerging results.

Emerging Regionalism

We are in the embryonic stage of regionalism, testing different approaches, ideas, and implementation strategies. In the past decade a range of regional strategies and design structures has evolved in several states across the country. One lesson is already clear: there is no one solution or ideal process. In each place differences in history, scale, ecology, geography, economics, and politics produce many forms of regionalism.

In all U.S. metropolitan areas, several regional institutions are already coordinating critical infrastructure, investments, and policy—but in piecemeal fashion. Regional transportation investments are already controlled by Metropolitan Planning Organizations (MPOs) as part of the process of allocating state and federal money. But these organizations have no control over the land-use patterns that drive the transportation demands—a key disconnect. Other single-purpose regional entities have evolved to deal with unique regional assets. A good example is the San Francisco Bay Area's Bay Conservation and Development Commission, which controls development along and in the bay. But land use typically remains the singular domain of local jurisdictions and is at the heart of the greatest controversy surrounding regionalism.

Many think that effective regional design implies a top-down approach. But regionalism does not imply that each town gives up land-use control. It does imply that a larger strategic plan be developed by all involved: local jurisdictions, environmentalists, business interests, developers, and so on. MPOs or regional civic and business groups in cooperation with local governments can establish broad policies, goals, and infrastructure criteria. The region can establish goals and policies in several key areas: preservation of open-space systems, efficiency of infrastructure, location of major job centers, transportation investments, and the fair distribution of affordable housing. Using these parameters, local governments can still design a unique plan that defines all the elements of its community: housing, circulation, open space, land use, urban design, and more.

In fact, without such regional policies, many local initiatives can be frustrated. For example, without regional open-space designations, individual towns may be unable to preserve the adjacent open-space systems they want. And clearly the major transportation improvements that cities need can only be coordinated at the regional level. Furthermore, regional policies to support reinvestment in lower-income communities may encourage redevelopment where local jurisdictions are unable to shift direction. The land-use decisions that complement such fundamental strategies must be adopted locally while they are coordinated regionally. No regional plan will succeed without local participation.

Oregon and Washington

Oregon and Washington provide alternate approaches to regional participation in land-use decisions. In Oregon a more top-down approach was implied in the creation of a regional government with district elections for local representation. This governing body has primary responsibility for the regional "Framework Plan" that sets overall growth, infrastructure, and land-use policies, as well as the placement of an Urban Growth Boundary (UGB).

Contrary to popular belief, the UGB in Oregon was not created to limit growth or stop sprawl but to protect farmlands from destabilizing land speculation. The 1972 legislation called for a boundary that would contain a twenty-year supply of developable land and for periodic line adjustments to ensure such capacity. Were it not for a 1992 regional visioning process, Metrovision 2040, the elastic UGB would have had little effect on outward growth. Metrovision 2040 organizers asked if the region should "grow up" or "grow out," and they engaged considerable community input. Given the choices and the trade-offs, the plan to "grow up" with more compact forms of development was selected by a wide margin.

The significant aspect of Oregon's growth management law is not that a top-down regional bureaucracy dictates land use to local governments but that the area must collectively analyze the impacts of future growth at a regional scale and come to a comprehensive decision about directions to take. When allowed to see clearly the impacts of more sprawl on their quality of life, the cost of infrastructure, and the impact to the environment, a majority of citizens opted for a more compact, transit-oriented growth pattern. These are trade-offs and choices people can make only when shown the cumulative impacts of different forms of growth at a regional scale.

In Washington the process started with, rather than resulted in, such a regional visioning effort. Called 2020 Vision, it produced a plan that configured the region with a hierarchy of centers and a complex set of growth boundaries that respected the needs and aspirations of individual communities. The plan was so successful that it led to state legislation for growth management. Under Washington's Growth Management Act, the local governments remain the proactive force in land-use decisions, with the regional entity acting primarily as a board of appeals. Local decisions can be challenged for either unreasonably breaching the UGB or undermining the general allocation of jobs and housing within each community. In other words, environmentalists have recourse if a district begins to sprawl beyond its growth boundary, and developers have recourse if NIMBYs constrain appropriate levels of development within the boundaries.

Maryland and Utah

Maryland's approach is different. It sets economic efficiency standards for public investments such as highway, sewer, water, housing, and economic development assistance. Rather than prescribe the location and pattern of development, the state's new "Neighborhood Conservation and Smart Growth Initiative" limits its investments in infrastructure to "priority funding areas." The concept is not to control the market or constrain private property rights but merely to spend public dollars cost-effectively. Significantly, the county governments, not the state, designate these areas. The areas, however, must meet several standards, such as a minimum density and coherent infrastructure plans, along with a demonstrated need for growth. Areas outside the priority areas can be developed but at the local government's or property owner's expense. This is a fair approach; the state seeks fiscal efficiency, and the private sector develops areas appropriate to the market. State subsidized land use is over.

Maryland has several other programs to protect open space and encourage job growth in existing centers. Its Rural Legacy Program uses sales tax dollars and bonds to purchase conservation easements for critical open space and farmlands. This program acknowledges that some lands would not be protected by the priority area designation alone. The Job Creation Tax Credit program provides tax benefits to employers who create jobs in the priority areas, and the Live Near Your Work program offers home-buying assistance to areas in which the employers are willing to provide matching assistance. The goal is to create more compact, efficiently served communities while preserving the state's open space and farmlands. These means form a sophisticated mix of incentives and limits that support reinvestment in the places that need it the most and avoid inefficient new infrastructure.

In Salt Lake City, a new initiative led by a civic group, Envision Utah, created alternative growth scenarios for their fast-growing area. For the projected one million population growth, they range from a compact transit-oriented alternative of 112 square miles of new development to a sprawling 439 in more standard forms. The infrastructure cost difference between the extremes was extraordinary, close to an additional $30,000 per new home. In addition, the low-density option did not meet the market demand for multifamily housing or first-time home buyers. This low-density option reflected a growing trend in the region's smaller suburban towns toward exclusionary zoning that allocated residential land primarily for large-lot single-family homes.

People tend to oppose denser development on a project-by-project basis, but when shown the cumulative loss of open space, affordable housing, and the additional tax burden at the regional scale, their response can be quite different. A mail-back survey included with a newspaper insert describing the Envision Utah alternatives showed that only 4 percent of the eighteen thousand respondents preferred the low-density growth alternate, while over 66 percent voted for the more compact alternatives. While many of these voters may have opposed higher-density development in their neighborhoods, the regional alternates process provided them a different perspective, one that has the power to reframe the issue and allow new preferences.

In addition, the respondents voted in similar proportions for more walkable forms of development with increased transit investments. The most preferred alternate matched the market demand for multifamily and small-home opportunities while reducing the average lot size of a single-family home by less than 20 percent. This option also placed three-fifths of the new residents within a half mile of rail transit stations and supported mixed-use neighborhoods that made walking convenient in 70 percent of the new development.

Since these alternates were analyzed and public preferences polled, the state legislators passed and the governor has signed the Quality Growth Act. Like the land management approach in Maryland, this legislation puts into place a commission to designate "quality growth" areas that will become the focus of new development and redevelopment. The state and federal government will make these areas priorities for new infrastructure and services. Other areas, although not specifically outside of a UGB, will have to pay their own development costs.

In addition, individual communities are following the regional plan on a volunteer basis. South Jordon, a town dominated by large-lot, single-family homes, approved a progressive mixed-use plan for ten thousand new homes in an area to be served by an extension of the light-rail line—at average densities twice that of their existing community. In addition, Kennecott Copper, the largest property holder in the region with over ninety thousand acres, is developing a plan based on the concepts of Transit-Oriented Development. And a recent study across multiple jurisdictions about adding a freeway on the west side of the valley included yet another transit line, along with appropriate land uses.

The most important aspect of each of these plans is the recognition that a definitive regional plan is a necessary step to a healthy future and that community participation is key to its success. When given clear information and a picture of the aggregate impacts of piecemeal growth, most citizens opt for very progressive policies. Seeing the growth in terms of its total impacts rather than one project at a time is a critical shift in perspective. Regional questions get different answers than local questions.

The Urban Network

Within these regional design efforts lies the need for a new model of mobility, a new vision of streets, arterials, and expressways that compliments the emerging land-use patterns. The movements of New Urbanism, Smart Growth, and Transit-Oriented Development have each defined these new, more compact, and walkable land-use forms. But too often the regional plans that call for New Urbanism and

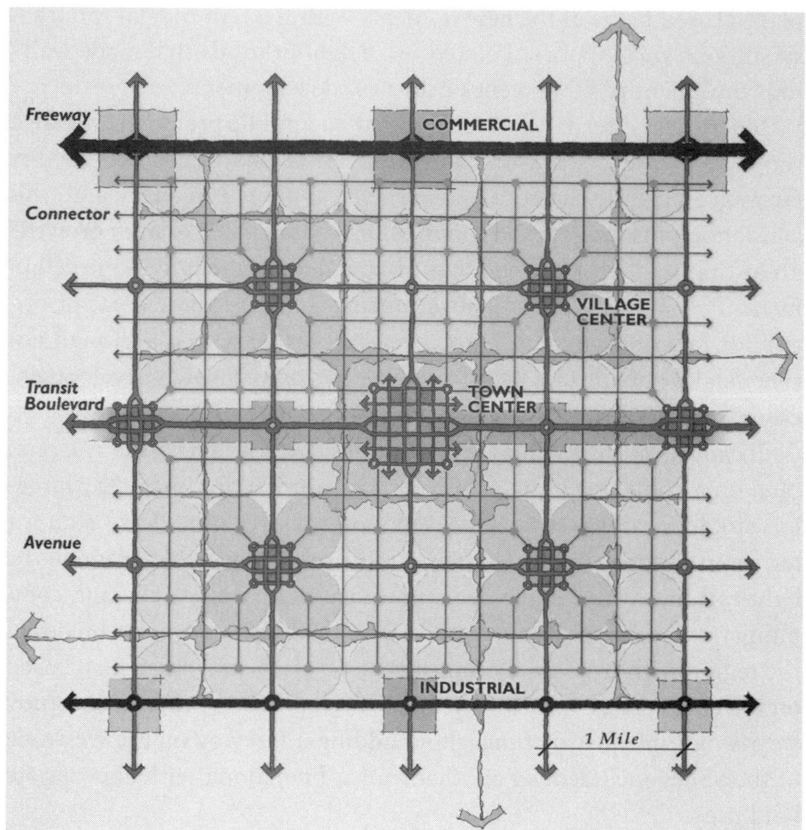

Calthorpe Associates, Urban Network diagram, 2005. The Urban Network integrates transportation and land use to create an internally consistent system. A well-connected street network greatly reduces the need for large streets that divide communities and create pedestrian barriers. Courtesy of Peter Calthorpe/Calthorpe Associates.

Smart Growth are forced to grow within a transportation network designed for sprawl. Our assumed transportation network is still a suburban grid of arterials punctuated with freeways.

A new circulation system to match the emerging mixed-use development patterns must be developed, one that accommodates mass transit as well as the car and that reinforces, rather than isolates, places that are walkable. Bringing daily destinations closer to home is a fundamental aspect of urbanism but is not the complete solution to our access needs. Even if we double the percentage of walkable trips in a neighborhood and triple transit ridership, there still will be growth in auto trips, not to mention an explosion of truck miles. We need a circulation system that accommodates all modes efficiently while it supports differing urban densities regionwide.

The old paradigm is simple: a grid of arterials spaced at one-mile increments with major retail centers located at the intersections and strip commercial buildings lining its inhospitable but very visible edges. Overlaying the grid in rings and radials is the freeway system. The intersection of the grid and freeway becomes fertile ground for malls and office parks. This formal system is rational, coherent, and true to itself, even if increasingly dysfunctional. Its sprawling land-use patterns match the road network in a way that New Urbanism, when dropped into this framework, cannot.

Our firm developed the concept of an Urban Network for Chicago Metropolis 2020, a private regional planning effort of the historic Commercial Club for the greater Chicago area. The Urban Network proposes three types of major roads to replace the standard arterial grid: Transit Boulevards, Avenues, and Connectors. The Transit Boulevards combine through auto trips with transit right-of-ways, the Avenues lead to local commercial destinations, and the Connectors provide circulation between neighborhoods.

The Transit Boulevards are at the heart of this network. They are multifunctional throughways designed to match the mixed-use urban development they support. Like traditional boulevards, they would have a central area for through traffic and transit, along with small-scale access roads on the sides to support local activities and a pedestrian environment. On Transit Boulevards, cafés, small businesses, apartments, transit, pedestrians, and through traffic mingle in a simple and time-tested hierarchy.

Transit Boulevards are lined with higher-density development and run to and through town centers. The key is a dedicated lane for the transit so that it can run at efficient speeds, and the small frontage road that supports the adjacent buildings and life of the sidewalk. This is in contrast to the typical arterial, which rarely provides space for transit or an edge treatment that encourages little other than strip commercial or sound walls.

The transit system running along the Boulevards and through the towns could be light-rail, streetcars, or bus rapid transit (BRT). When light-rail is not possible, the capital and operational costs of BRT are affordable and make it viable for widespread use. New, super-efficient natural-gas engines and advanced bus design would make buses reasonable companions to the environment of the Boulevard.

Avenues would intersect the Boulevards at one-mile centers. These Avenues would allow more frequent intersections, just as our existing suburban system does. However, at major intersections they can

Calthorpe Associates, Transit Boulevard, 2002. The Transit Boulevard serves multiple functions well, with transit and auto through traffic in the center, local traffic in access roads, and buildings facing the street. Courtesy of Peter Calthorpe/Calthorpe Associates.

support a Village Center—a mixed-use transformation of the typical grocery-store-anchored shopping center into a walkable community center. Between such centers, Avenues would have a parkway treatment and can be lined by alley-loaded, large-lot homes—as in the historic neighborhoods of many American cities.

Finally, a system of Connector streets forms a finer grid of approximately one-quarter-mile spacing, providing direct access to local village and town centers. These Connector streets replace the standard "collector streets," local streets with so much traffic that they are lined with sound walls and connect only to arterials. In contrast, the Connector streets are frequent enough to disperse the traffic so as to create livable environments along them. Because this street type allows direct access to village and town centers, it also relieves the Avenues of local trips, allowing fewer lanes.

A plan for the City of Merced, California, compared the old circulation patterns to the Urban Network for traffic performance. The Urban Network held the quantities of the various land uses constant while substituting Avenues at one-mile centers, a central Transit Boulevard for the standard arterials, and multiple continuous Connectors instead of collectors. The analysis showed a considerable drop in the volumes on the primary roads as local trips shifted to the Connectors. While the arterials system needed 75 percent four-lane and 25 percent six-lane facilities, the Urban Network needed no six-lane roads. More surprising was that in the standard system over 67 percent of the collectors carried over five thousand cars a day (more than one would wish to live next to), while the more frequent Connectors dispersed the traffic so that only 5 percent had that quantity.

In the old hierarchy of functional types, streets serve single functions. The new street types combine uses, capacities, and scales. For example the Transit Boulevards combine the capacity of a major arterial with the intimacy of local frontage roads and the pedestrian orientation that comes with its transit system. The Avenues are multilane roads that transition into a "couplet" of one-way main streets at the village centers. Streets, like land use, can no longer be single purpose, and they must change as they move through differing urban environments.

This new circulation system is combined with the new mixed-use land-use patterns of New Urbanism and Smart Growth. Walkable town and village centers are placed at the crossroads of Transit Boulevards and Avenues. Residential neighborhoods are directly accessible to these centers through local connector streets as well as the Avenues.

At such commercial centers, the Boulevard and Avenues would split into two one-way streets set a block apart, creating an urban grid of pedestrian-scaled streets. No street in such a town would contain more than three travel lanes (typically two), allowing pedestrian continuity without diverting auto capacity. In addition, this

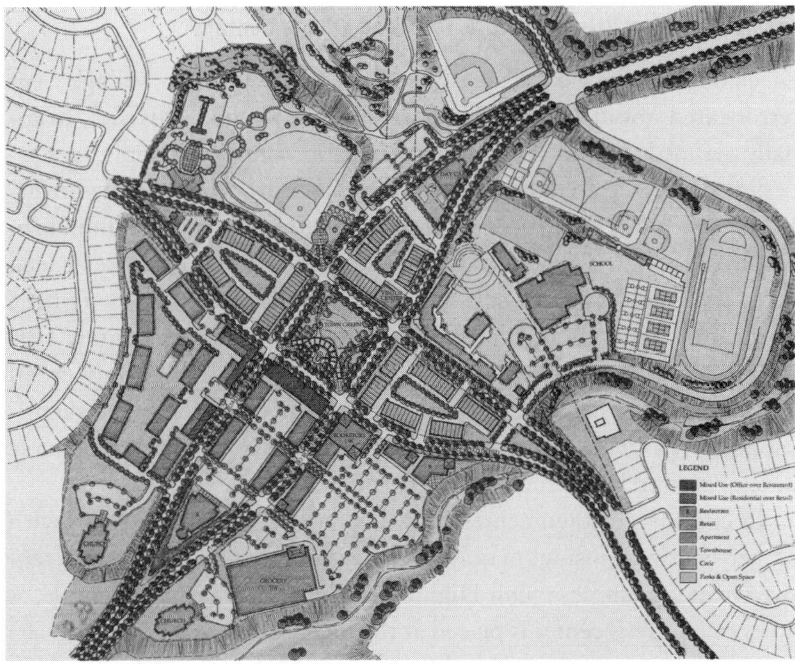

Calthorpe Associates, plan for San Elijo Hills Village Center, San Marcos, California, 2002. The couplet in this village center balances auto traffic with livability. The center contains a rich mix of commercial, residential, and civic uses in a walkable district. Courtesy of Peter Calthorpe/Calthorpe Associates.

one-way system eliminates left-turn delays, actually decreasing travel time for cars.

Each mixed-use place has an appropriate location, scale, and type of access. The larger town center is accessible to the Boulevard's plentiful through traffic and its high-capacity transit line. It mixes major employment with regional retail, major civic destinations, and high-density housing—essentially a suburban "Edge City" given urban and walkable configurations. Village centers contain what the International Council of Shopping Centers calls "neighborhood serving retail," typically anchored by a grocery store. They mix shops, a bit of office space, medium-density housing, and local civic uses. It typically takes four to six neighborhoods, each with a one-quarter-mile walking radius, to support a village center. The villages are directly accessible by foot, bus, car, or bike from surrounding neighborhoods along connector roads, while their couplet streets allow the auto traffic needed to support their retail.

Examples of New Urban Network Town and Village centers

An example of such a village center is the San Elijo Hills Village Center, located about forty miles north of San Diego. This site, originally planned around a standard intersection of two arterials, was redesigned to place a village green at the center of four one-way streets. In one quadrant, the grocery store anchors the primary retail; in others housing and civic buildings line the streets. Two main streets lead up to the green, and mixed-use buildings surround it. In two of the quadrants, a school and community park complete the center. This village center is now largely built and has been both a commercial and community success. Although the traffic engineers were skeptical at first, a detailed analysis proved the concept, and a visionary developer marshaled the concept through implementation.

In contrast, a town center contains much more retail along with higher-density housing, major office development, and a more extensive street system. Issaquah Highlands, thirty miles east of Seattle, is an example. This center is placed at the intersection of a major new arterial (projected to carry about fifty thousand vehicles per day to a new freeway interchange) and the entry to a new community with about forty-three hundred units of housing. Some five hundred more units are planned in the town center, along with nine hundred thousand square feet of retail and commercial space. In addition, the Microsoft Corporation has acquired part of the town center for a major office campus of about two million square feet.

Splitting the arterials into one-way couplets allowed an urban grid to organize the site and provided for a pedestrian-scaled environment even with the high traffic volumes. It effectively unified what would have been an isolated office park next to a shopping center. The standard arterial had a primary intersection with a 166-foot pedestrian crossing, while the couplets had two streets, one 40 feet wide and the other just 28 feet wide. The traffic engineers found that the auto travel time through the center was actually reduced by 11 percent compared to time through conventional intersections. In this case both the developer and Issaquah wanted a walkable, mixed-use town center and pressed the state highway department to allow the innovative road configuration. The project is now under construction, and the primary road network is complete.

Another example of a large-scale application of the Urban Network is the master plan for the twenty-thousand-acre St. Andrews expansion area north of Perth, Australia. In this case an enlightened metropolitan government seeking a transit-oriented community to anchor the northern quadrant of the region worked closely with a developer who shared this vision. The region had put in place urban design standards to insure mixed-use development, walkability, and a rigorous jobs/housing balance. This new town plan for 150,000 people and over 50,000 jobs shows a hierarchy of neighborhoods, villages, and two town centers set into an Urban Network with open-space systems preserving the coast and weaving through the community. In this example, the spacing and configuration of the Urban Network conform to environmental constraints and existing development.

The Urban Network also has a role to play in redeveloping areas. In such areas, existing suburban arterials can be converted into Transit Boulevards and lined with mixed-use development. In fact, the new regional plan for the Southern California Association of Governments envisions many of the major streets in the old arterial grid of Los Angeles converting to Transit Boulevards with a complement of higher-density development along the corridors. Wilshire Boulevard is the model for its highest-density expression. Ironically, many of these arterials were once home to streetcars prior to the Second World War.

Various cities are simultaneously up-zoning areas along the new transit boulevards and at light-rail stations. Malibu, Pasadena, and other smaller communities are planning for and building workable Transit-Oriented Developments. These dramatic changes come from the political awareness that more sprawl will not address the challenges the region confronts and are partly the result of new market forces calling for redevelopment, affordable housing, and transportation alternatives. In this case the preconceptions of sprawl are being overturned by a new paradigm of growth and a new set of investments, policies, and demographics. Los Angeles provided a test for the auto-oriented metropolis, and it will provide the test of its transformation.

It is shortsighted to think that significant changes in land use and regional structure can be realized without fundamentally reordering our transportation system. Only an integrated network of urban places and multiuse street systems can support the change needed for the next century of growth. The integration of these strategies forms a new paradigm of development—one that starts with new regional visions, reorders the policies and standards that underlie our infrastructure, and redirects the form of our neighborhoods and towns. It is an intentional and precisely designed system, just like the one it will replace.

There is no such thing as laissez-faire development. All development is planned, regulated, and subsidized. Consumer preference is shaped by history, opportunity, government policy, and expectations as much as by lifestyle needs or wants. Our choice is not between planning and laissez-faire but among different visions of community development and the physical structure and policies that underlie these visions.

11

Design by Deception: The Politics of Megaproject Approval

Bent Flyvbjerg

Some years ago, I was threatened by a high-ranking government official as I was beginning research on cost overruns in large construction projects. He told me in no uncertain terms that if I came up with results that reflected badly on his government and its projects, he would personally make sure my research funds dried up. I told him that he had just demonstrated that the research must be done and was likely to produce interesting results. The results are now being published, and if the official walks his talk, I am not likely to receive another research grant from his government.

The Machiavellian Formula for Project Approval

Which large projects get built? My research associates and I found it is not necessarily the best ones but instead those for which proponents best succeed in designing—deliberately or not—a fantasy world of underestimated costs, overestimated revenues, overvalued local development effects, and underestimated environmental impacts. Project approval in most cases depended on these factors.

Our survey, the first and largest of its kind, looked at three hundred projects in twenty countries.[1] Working from the observation that

Olympic Stadium, opening ceremony, 2004 Olympic Games, Athens, Greece, August 2004. Photograph copyright George Tiedermann/New Sport/Corbis.

"Princes who have achieved great things have been those . . . who have known how to trick men with their cunning, and who, in the end, have overcome those abiding by honest principles," Machiavelli seems to have been chief architect on these projects.[2] Many project proponents do not hesitate to use this approach, even if it means misleading lawmakers, the public, and the media about the true costs and benefits of projects. The result is an inverted Darwinism—an unhealthy "survival of the unfittest"—for large public works and other construction projects.

During project implementation, when fact overcomes fiction, the consequences are huge cost overruns, delays, missing revenues, crippling debt, and, to add insult to injury, often also negative environmental and social impacts. The misplaced investments, overspending, and financial problems are of Enron- and WorldCom-scandal magnitude, though much less transparent and harder to fix.

Cost Overruns, Benefit Shortfalls

The recent $4-billion cost overrun for the Pentagon spy satellite program and the over $5-billion overrun on the International Space Station are typical of defense and aerospace projects. But the problem is not limited to those programs. Examples from transport, the main focus of our study, include Boston's Big Dig, otherwise known as the Central Artery/Tunnel Project, which went 275 percent, or $11 billion, over budget in constant dollars.[3] Actual costs for Denver's $5-billion International Airport were close to 200 percent higher than estimated costs. The overrun on the new span of the San Francisco–Oakland Bay Bridge is currently $2.5 billion, or more than 100 percent over budget. The Los Angeles subway and many other urban rail projects worldwide have had similar overruns. The Chunnel between the United Kingdom and France came in 80 percent over budget for construction and 140 percent over for financing. At the initial public offering, Eurotunnel, the private owner of the tunnel, lured investors by telling them that 10 percent "would be a reasonable allowance for the possible impact of unforeseen circumstances on construction costs."[4] Anybody familiar with the risks involved in projects of this kind would have known this to be deceptive underestimation aimed at selling shares in the tunnel.

Our studies show that transportation projects, public buildings, power plants, dams, water projects, sports stadiums, oil and gas extraction projects, information technology systems, aerospace projects, and weapons systems follow a general pattern of cost underestimation and overrun.[5] Many such projects end up financial disasters. Unfortunately, the consequences are not always only financial, as is illustrated by the NASA space shuttle. Here, the cooking of budgets to make this underperforming project look good on paper has been linked with shortchanged safety upgrades related to the deaths of seven astronauts aboard the Columbia shuttle in 2003.

As for benefit shortfalls, consider Bangkok's US$2-billion SkyTrain, a two-track elevated urban rail system that looks like a prop from *Blade Runner* and is designed to service some of the most densely populated areas from the air. The first time you try to ride the train, you may wonder why the cars stop far down the track from you. The explanation is that the system is greatly oversized, with station platforms too long for its shortened trains. Many trains and cars sit in the garage. Why? Because actual traffic turned out to be less than half that forecast.[6] Every effort has been made to market and promote the train, but the project company has ended up in financial trouble. Even though urban rail is probably a good idea for a dense, congested, and air-polluted city like Bangkok, overinvesting in idle capacity is hardly the best way to use resources, especially in a developing nation in which capital for investment is particularly scarce. Such benefit shortfalls are common and have also haunted the Channel tunnel, the Los Angeles subway, and Denver's International Airport.

The list of projects designed with cost overruns and/or benefit shortfalls seems endless. In North America: the F/A-22 fighter aircraft; FBI's Trilogy information system; Ontario's Pickering nuclear plant; subways in numerous cities, including Miami and Mexico City; convention centers in Houston, Los Angeles, and other cities; the Animas–La Plata water project; the Sacramento regional sewer system renewal; the Quebec Olympic stadium; Toronto's SkyDome; the Washington Public Power Supply System; and the Iraq reconstruction effort. In Europe: the Eurofighter military jet, the new British Library, the Millennium Dome, the Nimrod maritime patrol plane, the U.K. West Coast rail upgrade and the related Railtrack fiscal collapse, the Astute attack submarine, the Humber Bridge, the Tyne metro system, the Scottish parliament building, the French Paris Nord TGV, the Berlin–Hamburg maglev train, Hanover's Expo 2000, Russia's Sakhalin-1 oil and gas project, Norway's Gardermo airport, the Øresund Bridge between Sweden and Denmark, the Great Belt rail tunnel linking Scandinavia with continental Europe, and the Copenhagen Metro. In Australasia: Sydney's Olympic stadiums, Japan's Joetsu Shinkansen high-speed rail line, India's Sardar Sarovar dams, the Surat-Manor tollway project, Calcutta's metro, and Malaysia's Pergau dam.[7] I could go on.

Job creation and other local economic benefits invariably used by proponents to justify the billions spent on such projects often do not materialize or are so weak that they cannot be measured outside of the temporary jobs generated by construction itself, which may be substantial, but the benefits of which end the day the last construction worker leaves the site. Even for a giant project like the Channel tunnel, which is several times the size of most megaprojects, studies show that five years after the tunnel's opening it had had very few and very small impacts on the wider economy. Additionally, it was difficult to identify any major urban or regional developments associated with it, and potential impacts on the directly affected regions were found to be mainly negative.[8] Studies of other projects corroborate these findings: the much-publicized positive economic and regional development effects of large construction projects are mostly nonexistent, marginal, or even negative.[9] This does not mean that transportation hubs and highways exits do not affect the location of development. But the net effect on economic development, if it exists, is difficult to measure.

In developing nations, large dams are the classical example of underperforming projects with negative social and environmental impacts often not outweighed by positive development impacts.[10] The Sardar Sarovar and Maheshwar dams in India are particularly well known because of author Arundhati Roy's vivid descriptions in *The Cost of Living* and *The Algebra of Infinite Justice* of the human suffering resulting from these projects.[11] Many other examples exist, including the Three Gorges Dam in China and the Pergau Dam in Malaysia. A number of case studies of smaller but still large urban infrastructure and services projects in Pakistan, Bangladesh, India, and Ethiopia show similar results: pre-project social impact analysis cannot be trusted, the poor are not considered, and hundreds of thousands of livelihoods are disrupted or lost with no immediate prospect for reemployment.[12] This does not mean that such projects should not be undertaken. It does mean, however, that projects should have much more realistic predictions of costs and impacts before decisions are made and much better practices of participation with and compensation for those negatively affected.

Every large construction project does not follow the pattern of

Mott MacDonald, Bridge to Chek Lap Kok Airport Project, Lantau Island, Hong Kong, ca. June 1996. Photograph copyright Michael Yamashita/Corbis.

understated costs and overstated benefits, needless to say. But most do. Nine times out of ten, in the projects we studied, costs begin to soar after projects have been approved, leaving taxpayers or investors to pick up bills of hundreds of millions of dollars. Cost overruns of 50 percent are common. Overruns above 100 percent are not uncommon.[13] Of a sample of forty projects for which it was possible to establish reliable data on both costs and revenues, only one project had costs that had been overestimated and revenues that had been underestimated by more than 20 percent, whereas the opposite was true for thirty-four projects: for each, costs were underestimated and benefits overestimated by more than 20 percent. Only five of the forty projects had actual costs and revenues less than 20 percent different from forecasted costs and revenues. For rail projects, for example, half of all projects have cost overruns of 45 percent or more, measured in constant dollars. When this is combined with lack of traveler use, which for half of all rail projects is more than 50 percent lower than forecasted, it becomes clear why so many projects have financial problems.

The Master Builder Who Didn't Build

Some argue that almost no projects, including our most treasured ones, would ever be undertaken if some form of delusion about costs and benefits were not involved. The Brooklyn Bridge, for instance, had a cost overrun of 100 percent, the Sydney Opera House of 1,400 percent. Had the true costs been known, these architectural wonders might not have been built. Delusion is necessary for action—and for exquisite design—according to this argument.

Michael Teitz and Andrejs Skaburskis follow this line of reasoning when they ask of the Sydney Opera House, for which promoters gave a deceptively low budget to ensure political acceptance, "Did people really think that the Sydney Opera House would come in on budget? Or did we all agree to accept the deception and engage in wishful thinking in order to make something that we really wanted happen? . . . [D]o Australians really regret those dramatic sails in the harbour? Or would they have regretted more the decision that would most reasonably have been based on a fair prediction of costs?"[14] The logic is seductive yet precarious. I have the highest appreciation of the Sydney Opera House and especially for its architect, Jørn Utzon, who is an honorary professor at Aalborg University, where I work. Such appreciation is easy when you live in the childhood hometown of the man, next door to the Utzon Center, and close to several of the few Utzon designs that have been built.

It seems to me, however, that one does Utzon and other architects a disservice if one indicates that their work could be built only through deception or wishful thinking, while similarly iconic and complex designs did not require this, for instance, Frank Gehry's Guggenheim Museum Bilbao, which was built on time and budget and makes a lot more money than projected.[15] What would explain this difference? And how would we distinguish, when planning such treasures, between those that in order to happen need deception and those that do not? And all this does not take into consideration the fact that in most nations deliberate deception about publicly funded projects is considered unethical and is illegal.

What is more, the real loss in the Sydney Opera House project is not the huge cost overrun in itself. It is that the overrun and the controversy it created kept Utzon from building more masterpieces. In a meeting held in support of Utzon at Sydney Town Hall in March 1966—six weeks before the controversy made Utzon leave Sydney and the Opera House—the Viennese-born Australian architect Harry Seidler said, "If Mr. Utzon leaves, a crime will have been committed against future generations of Australians. . . ."[16] Seidler was more right than he could imagine, except the crime would not be limited to future generations of Australians. After winning the Pritzker Prize in 2003, Utzon is again widely acclaimed, even in Australia. But he was not able to build for decades. Instead of having a whole oeuvre to enjoy—like those of Frank Lloyd Wright and Gehry—we have just one main building. Utzon was thirty-eight when he won the competition for the Opera House—how would the work of the mature master have enriched our lives? We will never know. That is the high price Sydney has imposed by its incompetence in building the Opera House. And even if the Opera House is an extreme case and other famous architects got more commissions after going over budget, Sydney drives home an important point: cost underestimation is disruptive, sometimes in drastic and unexpected ways.

For these reasons, we should be wary of promoting the argument that deception and delusion are good because they make things happen, including great design. Many viable projects exist—in public buildings, transport, energy, sports, and tourism—that have not required deception: in addition to the Guggenheim Museum Bilbao, for the Pompidou Center, the Empire State Building, and the Eiffel Tower, cost projections were reliable.

The Guggenheim Museum Bilbao and the Sydney Opera House Compared

Frank Gehry has a reputation for building on time and budget, even for large, complex, and innovative structures. I asked Gehry how he and his associates do it. Gehry explained that the first step is to ensure that what he calls the "organization of the artist" prevails during construction.[17] According to Gehry, the goal is to prevent political and business interests from interfering with design and thus to arrive at an outcome as close as possible to the original design drawings. Gehry explains:

> One of the great failings in these public projects is public clients, that is, clients that are involved with politics and business interests. These clients often eliminate good architecture because they don't understand it, and they're wary of it, and they're unable to imagine that somebody who looks like an artist could possibly be responsible. There's a tendency to marginalize and treat the creative people like women are treated, "sweetie, us big business guys know how to do this, just give us the design and we'll take it from there." That is the worst thing that can happen. It requires the organization of the artist to prevail so that the end product is as close as possible to the object of desire that both the client and architect have come to agree on.

Once the design has been agreed on and the organization of the artist-architect set up, the next step in building on time and budget is to get a realistic cost estimate and control it. Gehry explains the difficulty of this:

> Building costs are not as controllable as people make them sound. . . . You might have a project that you believe is budgeted properly and has been assessed by other responsible assessors to be within budget, a change in the market throws it all out of whack right in the middle of your process, so there is no guarantee, ever. The only way to control these things is to not proceed with the building until you have all the drawings complete, you have everything the way you want it, you've done your due diligence on cost

> analysis. Then it's a negotiation from there on with contractors and sub-contractors to keep them within your budget.

Finally, technology and continuing relationships with the individual building trades are important ingredients in keeping within budgets, says Gehry. He and his associates have pioneered the use of digital design models that greatly facilitate production of the data needed for arriving at accurate budgets. Here, Gehry also argues that construction should not start until it has been established that a project is indeed within the client's budget:

> In our practice we don't allow the client to start construction until we are sure we are doing a building that's within their budget and meets their requirements. We use all the technology available to us to quantify in a most precise way the elements of the building. This fact alone allows us to demystify for the construction people the elements of the building so there's not a lot of guessing. When there's guessing, money is added. We found that precision in documentation and continuing relationships with the individual building trades is a necessary process to keep buildings within the limits of the client's budget.

This explains how the Guggenheim Museum Bilbao was built on time and budget. Compare this with what happened in Sydney. Point by point the approach was exactly opposite.

In Sydney, the original budget of 7 million Australian dollars was not a real but a political budget. The Labour government of New South Wales, the main proponent of the Opera House, wanted the project approved and construction started before elections in March 1959—this would reduce the risk of the Opera House being stopped in case Labour lost the elections.[18] A lowballed budget and a fast-track start-up were means to this end. The premier, Joe Cahill, had made the Opera House his personal priority, but he was seriously ill and running out of time. According to Bob Carr, New South Wales premier since 1995, Cahill told his people, "I want you to go down to Bennelong Point [the location of the Opera House site] and make such progress that no one who succeeds me can stop this going through to completion."[19] Construction started before either drawings or funds were fully available. If one principal cause is identified for the troubles that beset the Opera House, this is it. Eventually the Opera House would cost 102 million Australian dollars, not including 45 million dollars allocated in 2002 in part to bring the building more in agreement with Utzon's original designs. Kim Utzon explains in lieu of his father, who prefers to remain out of the public eye:[20] "It was a political decision to publicize a low budget for the building, which was expected to gain approval in the political system, but which very quickly was exceeded. So even if the cost overrun turned out to be 1,400 percent in relation to the publicized budget, this budget was an eighth of the real budget for the building. So the real cost overrun is only 100 percent. The rest was politics."

Second, what Gehry calls the "organization of the artist" was not implemented in Sydney. The political and business interests that Gehry says must be kept at arm's length from design got deeply involved. The political trick played with the falsely low initial budget kept haunting construction as an endless series of cost overruns that were not all real overruns but logical consequences of cost underestimation. After the Sydney Opera House Act was approved in 1960 with the provision that every 10 percent increase in the budget would require the act to be amended by Parliament, the Opera House became a political football. Every overrun now set off an increasingly menacing debate about the emerging structure in Sydney Harbor. The architect inevitably became a target. He was said to have "lousy taste," and his design was called "something that is crawling out of the ocean with nothing good in mind" and "copulating white turtles."[21] When even the government of New South Wales began to attack Utzon and stopped paying his fees and claims, the debate began to look to Utzon like a campaign to drive him off the project. In April 1966, he secretly left Australia with his family, swearing never to return. Not only was Sydney not able to keep the organization of the artist in place, it was unable to keep the artist. Kim Utzon explains:

> They were a few years from completing the building [when Jørn Utzon left]; the detailed drawings and plans were all completed, and major parts had been built. Much of it was then torn out of the house again in order to change things. For instance, a full revolving stage and a full rigging loft delivered from Germany were removed. They also dynamited part of the structure in order to create space for more seats, from which, by the way, you cannot see the stage. So many errors were made, and one of them was to change architects halfway through construction. The main cause of the change of architects was the falsely low and political initial budget and the

cost overruns it created. But then the change of architects produced its own overruns.

The evidence supports Kim Utzon's claims. Large cost increases took place after Utzon left.[22] And contemporary architectural critics have pointed out that due to the changes in the original design, the building's interior is no match for the exterior. What is worse, although the building works well for rock concerts, movie performances, conventions, and chamber orchestras, because of the changes, it is unsuited for classical operas.[23] This would seem to be a major drawback for an opera house, and in a postscript to this amazing story, in 2001, thirty-five years after he left Australia, Jørn Utzon was invited back to help restore the building and secure its future more in accordance with his original designs. Utzon accepted the invitation.

Finally, in the late 1950s and early 1960s Utzon did not have access to the design technology and computing power available to Gehry in the 1990s. Consequently, Utzon and his engineers had great difficulty finding a practical way of building the curved concrete shell vaults. Nothing worked until, after several years of experimentation, the team hit upon the now famous "orange peel" simplification. The surfaces of the shells were defined as triangular patches of different sizes on the surface of a single sphere, like pieces of an orange peel. This allowed exact calculation and the use of prefabricated repeating elements, reducing costs to more acceptable levels.[24] Even so, the years of experimentation translated into years of delay, which again translated into cost overruns.

Gehry's initial sketches and models for the Guggenheim Museum Bilbao were, if anything, more daring in their use of free-form curved surfaces than Utzon's. But now accurate modeling was no longer a problem. Gehry's office employed Catia, an advanced CAD system mostly used, until then, in aerospace and automobile design.[25] Whereas Utzon had been forced to rely on painstakingly handmade drawings and models in his explorations of structure, Gehry could employ visualization software to create, almost instantly, whatever views he needed. He could also use rapid prototyping tools to produce physical models automatically. But most important, the digital model provided the data needed for the "precision in documentation" Gehry says is crucial for estimating and controlling costs correctly and thus keeping what he calls "good architecture" at arm's length from controversy and political debate.

In sum, by enforcing "the organization of the artist," by accurate budgeting and cost control, and by using advanced computing technology, Bilbao gained a building that works as an art museum, as a work of art in its own right, as a business, as a much-needed development vehicle for the Basque region, and as a source of inspiration for lovers of good architecture and good city and regional planning everywhere. Sydney, by doing the opposite on all counts, got an opera house unsuited for opera. The part of the building that Utzon got to finish—the outside—is as iconic, to be sure, as the museum in Bilbao. The shells in Sydney Harbor have placed Australia on the global map like nothing else. But given the costs involved—the destruction of the career and oeuvre of an undisputed master of twentieth-century architecture—Sydney provides a lesson in what not to do.

The Lying Game

Proponents of the Sydney Opera House intentionally deceived lawmakers, the public, and the media when they lowballed the budget to get the project started. But is such behavior really common for large projects? And is Gehry's approach, as described above, the exception? Such questions are rarely asked. Maybe because in an uncomfortable number of cases the answer is "Yes." Our data show that the conventional explanations—the inherent difficulty of forecasting, inadequate data, inappropriate forecasting models—do not explain forecasting outcomes well. The outcomes are too biased, with nine out of ten cost forecasts being cost underestimates. The conventional explanations could be upheld only if outcomes were more normally distributed around a figure for error closer to zero. With an unusually high level of statistical significance, this is not the pattern that outcomes follow. Even more remarkably, for more than seventy years, cost overruns have stayed large and mainly constant—they are highly predictable.[26] But cost forecasters keep ignoring this, even though it could be used to make their forecasts much more accurate.[27] The situation is similar for forecasts of benefits.

Either the people who forecast are incredibly incompetent, which is unlikely, or they are incredibly optimistic, which is more common but still does not adequately explain the data. Again, many forecasters deliberately manipulate costs and benefits to help projects get approved. This best explains the data and has been further verified through interviews with forecasters and planners conducted by both my own research teams and by others.[28] For reasons of space, I include but one example of a planner explaining the mechanism of cost underestimation in an interview: "You will often as a planner know the real costs [of projects]. You know that the budget is too low, but it is difficult to pass such a message to the counselors [politicians] and the private actors. They know that high costs reduce the chances of national funding."[29] In comparison, it is hard to imagine a society that would allow medical doctors to make the same predictable "errors" decade after decade in diagnosing and treating patients. This would be blatant malpractice. So it is in planning and design.

But what is most disturbing is not deceptive individual project estimates, it is the massive extent to which rent-seeking behavior by stakeholders has hijacked and replaced the pursuit of public good in this important and expensive policy area and the high costs this behavior imposes on society. Deceptive cost-benefit analyses keep critical scrutiny (by lawmakers, the public, and the media), accountability, and good governance at bay until it is too late, that is, until the sunk costs for a project are so high that its point of no return has been reached and construction must be completed. Thus, there are few half-built bridges and tunnels in the world, although there are many that function poorly.

Public planning—to deserve its name—presupposes a notion of public good. When this notion is hijacked, planning itself is hijacked. Instead we get one of the most undermining misfits of democracy: the public institution used for private gain. Any society that wants to remain one will have to prevent such hijacking and restore the vital distinction between public good and private interest. The same may be said of planning: The public good, as defined by law, is planning's raison d'être.

But the whole structure of incentives for planning major projects is geared toward keeping deception going. Each project is a multimillion- and often even multibillion-dollar business, and when it goes forward, many people profit—architects, engineers, contractors, consultants, bankers, landowners, construction workers, lawyers, and developers. In addition, politicians with a "monument complex" gain satisfaction and get to cut ribbons, administrators get larger budgets, and cities get investments and infrastructures that might otherwise go elsewhere. Stakeholders may have an interest in letting a project go ahead even if it is not especially useful from a public point of view.

Corruption also plays a role. According to Transparency International, the frequency and size of bribes are higher in construction and public works than in any other economic sector. This holds true in both developed and developing nations. On a scale from 0 to 10, with 0 indicating the highest possible level of corruption, construction and public works scored 1.3.[30] The problem is amplified by the scale of construction expenditures, which are estimated at US$3,200 billion per year worldwide.[31] Transparency International emphasizes that the majority of those who engage in corrupt practices do not do so because they wish to, but because they feel compelled to by the modus operandi of the construction industry and the political environment. In many contexts, bribes are expected and needed to get projects built.

Finally, the incentive to propose new projects has grown stronger over time for the simple reason that taxes have gradually increased over the past several decades in most nations, in both absolute terms and as a share of GDP, despite all the rhetoric about privatization and lean government.[32] This is the so-called honey-pot effect. Major public works projects are effective in extracting honey from the pot.

Undoubtedly, many project proponents believe that their projects will benefit society and that, consequently, they are warranted in cooking up costs and benefits—just as executives at Enron and WorldCom believed they were justified in cooking the books for the good of the company. The ends justify the means, or so the players reason. Together with the strong incentives to propose and build projects, this means that something more insidious than simple, individual deception may be at play: a whole culture of covert deceit.

As was pointed out in an editorial in *Access* magazine, few of the players involved are likely to think of themselves as dishonest or corrupt.[33] It might seem odd that low-cost, high-benefit forecasts miraculously and repeatedly fit clients' and forecasters' silent wishes. But their wishes may not be questioned. Rather, it is taken for granted by politicians, stakeholders, and the media that the proposed highway, concert hall, bridge, stadium, dam, or rail line is the correct answer to the problem, and cost-benefit estimates somehow come out just right. Like patriotism, forecasters' conviction requires no rationale and brooks no serious doubt. Projects follow under their own momentum. As in any other culture in which critical voices are suppressed, eventually the dominant players begin to believe in their own deceptions, reinforcing their feeling of being justified.

Reform, Please

As should be clear, the planning and implementation of major construction projects stand in need of reform. Fortunately, help is coming. The conventional consensus that deception and even corruption are acceptable ways of getting projects started is under attack, as will be apparent from the examples below. This is in part because democratic governance is generally getting stronger around the world. The Enron scandal and its successors have triggered a war on corporate deception that is spilling over into government with the same objective: to curb huge financial waste. Although progress is slow, democratic governance is gaining a foothold even in major project development. The conventional consensus is also under attack for the practical reason that megaprojects are becoming so large in relation to national economies that cost overruns and benefit shortfalls from even a single project may destabilize the finances of a whole country or region. This happened when the billion-dollar cost overrun of the 2004 Athens Olympics affected the credit rating of Greece. It was also the case when Hong Kong's new $20-billion Chek Lap Kok airport opened in 1998. Lawmakers and governments are beginning to see that national fiscal distress is too high a price to pay for the megaprojects lying game and that reform is needed.

In 2003 the Treasury of the United Kingdom required, for the first time, that all ministries develop and implement procedures for large public projects that will curb what it calls—with true British civility—"optimism bias." Funding will be unavailable for projects that do not take into account this bias, and methods have been developed for how to do this.[34] In the Netherlands in 2004, the Parliament Committee on Infrastructure Projects for the first time conducted extensive public hearings to identify measures that will limit the misinformation about large infrastructure projects given to the Parliament, public, and media. In Boston, the government sued to recoup funds from contractor overcharges for the Big Dig related to cost overruns. More governments and parliaments are likely to follow the lead of the United Kingdom, the Netherlands, and Boston in coming years. It is too early to tell whether the measures they implement will ultimately be effective. It seems unlikely, however, that the forces that have triggered the measures will be reversed.

The key weapons in the war on deception are accountability and critical questioning. The professional expertise of planners, architects, engineers, economists, and administrators is certainly indispensable to constructing the buildings and infrastructures that make society work. Our studies show, however, that the claims about costs and benefits made by these groups usually cannot be trusted and should be carefully examined by independent specialists and organizations. The same holds for claims made by project-promoting politicians and officials. Institutional checks and balances—including financial, professional, or even criminal penalties for consistent and unjustifiable biases in claims and estimates of costs and benefits—should be developed and employed. Elsewhere, my research group and I have shown in detail how this may be done.[35] The key principle is that the cost of making a wrong forecast should fall on those making the forecast, a principle often violated today.

Many of the public-private partnerships currently emerging in large construction projects contain more and better checks and balances than previous institutional setups, as has been demonstrated by the U.K. National Audit Office.[36] This is a step in the right direction but should be no cause for repose. The lying game has long historical roots and is deeply ingrained in professional and institutional practices. It would be naive to think it is easily toppled. Given the stakes involved—saving taxpayers from billions of dollars of waste, protecting citizens' trust in democracy and the rule of law, avoiding the destruction of great design and great designers—this should not deter us from trying.

Notes

1. Bent Flyvbjerg, Nils Bruzelius, and Werner Rothengatter, *Megaprojects and Risk: An Anatomy of Ambition* (Cambridge: Cambridge University Press, 2003); Bent Flyvbjerg, Mette K. Skamris Holm, and Søren L. Buhl, "Underestimating Costs in Public Works Projects: Error or Lie?" *Journal of the American Planning Association* 68, no. 3 (Summer 2002): 279–95; Bent Flyvbjerg, Mette K. Skamris Holm, and Søren L. Buhl, "What Causes Cost Overrun in Transport Infrastructure Projects?" *Transport Reviews* 24, no. 1 (January 2004): 3–18.

2. Niccolò Machiavelli, *The Prince,* trans. George Bull (Harmondsworth: Penguin, 1984 [1532]), 99.

3. For this and other figures of cost overruns, see Flyvbjerg, Bruzelius, and Rothengatter, *Megaprojects and Risk.*

4. "Under Water Over Budget," *Economist,* October 7, 1989, 37–38.

5. Flyvbjerg, Bruzelius, and Rothengatter, *Megaprojects and Risk,* 18–19. Flyvbjerg, Skamris Holm, and Buhl, "Underestimating Costs in Public Works Projects," 279–95.

6. Bent Flyvbjerg, Mette K. Skamris Holm, and Søren L. Buhl, "How (In)accurate Are Demand Forecasts in Public Works Projects? The Case of Transportation," paper accepted for publication in *Journal of the American Planning Association.*

7. Bent Flyvbjerg and Dan Lovallo, "Delusion and Deception: Two Models for Explaining Executive Disaster," paper in progress.

8. Roger Vickerman, "Long-Term Impacts of the Channel Tunnel: Methodology and Evidence," paper for *International Research Seminar on the Regional Development Impacts of the Øresund Bridge,* Copenhagen, November 28–29, 1999.

9. Flyvbjerg, Bruzelius, and Rothengatter, *Megaprojects and Risk,* 65–72.

10. Patrick McCully, *Silenced Rivers: The Ecology and Politics of Large Dams* (London: Zed Books, 2001); World Commission on Dams, *Dams and Development: A New Framework for Decision-Making* (London and Sterling, VA: Earthscan Publications, 2000).

11. Arundhati Roy, *The Cost of Living* (New Delhi: Penguin India, 2002); Arundhati Roy, *The Algebra of Infinite Justice* (New York: Modern Library, 1999).

12. Water Engineering and Development Centre, "Livelihood Substitution: Involving the Poor in Urban Infrastructure and Services Development," research project reported at http://wedc.lboro.ac.uk/index.php.

13. Flyvbjerg, Bruzelius, and Rothengatter, *Megaprojects and Risk,* 11–21.

14. Andrejs Skaburskis and Michael B. Teitz, "Forecasts and Outcomes," *Planning Theory and Practice* 4, no. 4 (December 2003): 429–42.

15. Personal communications with design architect Frank O. Gehry and executive architect Luis Rodriguez, author's archives.

16. Peter Murray, *The Saga of Sydney Opera House: The Dramatic Story of the Design and Construction of the Icon of Modern Australia* (London and New York: Spon Press, 2004), 105.

17. All quotes are from the author's personal communication with Frank Gehry, author's archives.

18. Murray, *The Saga of Sydney Opera House,* 21–22.

19. Australian Broadcasting Corporation, "Lateline," January 9, 2003, television program transcript, http://www.abc.nte.au/lateline/content/2003/s936770.htm.

20. All quotes are from the author's personal communication with Kim Utzon, author's archives.

21. Klaus Reichold and Bernhard Graf, *Buildings That Changed the World* (Munich: Prestel, 2004), 168.

22. Murray, *The Saga of Sydney Opera House,* xii–xiii.

23. Reichold and Graf, *Buildings That Changed the World,* 168.

24. William J. Mitchell, "A Tale of Two Cities: Architecture and the Digital Revolution," *Science* 285 (August 6, 1999): 839–40.

25. Ibid., 840–41.

26. Flyvbjerg, Skamris Holm, and Buhl, "Underestimating Costs in Public Works Projects," 285–87.

27. Bent Flyvbjerg, Carsten Glenting, and Arne Kvist Rønnest, *Procedures for Dealing with Optimism Bias in Transport Planning: Guidance Document* (London: UK Department for Transport, June 2004), 28–35.

28. Ibid., 36–58. Martin Wachs, "When Planners Lie with Numbers," *Journal of the American Planning Association* 55, no. 4 (Autumn 1989): 476–79; Martin Wachs, "Ethics and Advocacy in Forecasting for Public Policy," *Business and Professional Ethics Journal* 9, no. 1, 2 (Spring/Summer 1990): 141–57.

29. Flyvbjerg, Glenting, and Rønnest, *Procedures for Dealing with Optimism Bias in Transport Planning,* 44.

30. Transparency International, "Corruption in Construction," paper in progress, undated, 1–2.

31. Ibid.

32. Organisation for Economic Co-operation and Development (OECD), "Recent Tax Policy Trends and Reforms in OECD Countries," OECD Tax Policy Studies, no. 9, November 2004, 15–30.

33. Luci Yamamoto, "No Lying Game," *Access* 21 (Fall 2002): 1.

34. Mott MacDonald, *Review of Large Public Procurement in the UK,* study for HM Treasury (London: HM Treasury, July 2002); HM Treasury, *The Green Book: Appraisal and Evaluation in Central Government,* Treasury Guidance (London: TSO, 2003); Flyvbjerg, Glenting, and Rønnest, *Procedures for Dealing with Optimism Bias in Transport Planning.*

35. Flyvbjerg, Bruzelius, and Rothengatter, *Megaprojects and Risk,* 107–35.

36. National Audit Office, *PFI: Construction Performance* (London: National Audit Office, 2003), report by the Comptroller and Auditor General, HC 371 Session 2002–2003: February 5, 2003.

Contributors

Jonathan Barnett, FAIA, FAICP, is professor of practice in city and regional planning and director of the urban design program at the University of Pennsylvania. He is an urban designer at Wallace Roberts and Todd, LLC, Philadelphia, and author of *Redesigning Cities* and other books.

Lynn Becker writes on architecture for *Chicago Reader.* He is a lifelong resident of Chicago and an avid student of its architecture and of the personalities, politics, and processes behind its evolution.

Peter Calthorpe is principal of Calthorpe Associates, Berkeley, California, and author or coauthor of *The Regional City, The Next American Metropolis,* and other books.

Susan S. Fainstein is professor in the urban planning program at the Graduate School of Architecture, Planning, and Preservation at Columbia University. She is author of *The City Builders: Property Development in New York and London, 1980–2000,* among other books.

Bent Flyvbjerg, principal author of *Megaprojects and Risk,* is professor of planning and director of the research program on large infrastructure projects at Aalborg University in Denmark. He has served as an international advisor to governments, general auditors, and private companies for major projects.

Alexander Garvin is president and CEO of Alex Garvin and Associates, Inc. He was managing director of planning for New York City's committee for the 2012 Olympic bid. He has been vice president for planning, design, and development at the Lower Manhattan Development Corporation, the agency charged with redevelopment of the World Trade Center following 9/11. He is also adjunct professor of urban planning and management at Yale University.

John Kaliski, AIA, is principal of Urban Studio, Los Angeles, an architecture firm that has completed a wide range of urban design projects. He is adjunct faculty in design at the College of Environmental Design, California State Polytechnic University.

Jerold S. Kayden is Frank Backus Williams Professor of Urban Planning and Design and director of the master in urban planning degree program at Harvard University Graduate School of Design. He is author of *Privately Owned Public Space*, coauthor of *Landmark Justice*, and coeditor of *Zoning and the American Dream*.

Matthew J. Kiefer is a land-use and development attorney at Goulston and Storrs in Boston. He teaches in the urban planning program at the Harvard University Graduate School of Design.

Hubert Murray is principal of Hubert Murray Architect + Planner, Cambridge, and was chief architect on the Central Artery Project from 1989 to 1992.

Richard Plunz is professor of architecture and director of the urban design program at Columbia University. Among his books are *Housing Form and Public Policy in the United States*; *A History of Housing in New York City*; *Dwelling Type and Social Change in the American Metropolis*; *The Urban Lifeworld*; and *After Shopping*.

Leonie Sandercock is professor of urban planning and social policy, associate director of School of Community and Regional Planning, and chair of the Ph.D. program in planning at the University of British

Columbia. She is author of *Property, Politics, and Urban Planning*; *Towards Cosmopolis*; and *Cosmopolis II*; and editor of *Making the Invisible Visible*.

William S. Saunders is editor of *Harvard Design Magazine*, assistant dean at Harvard University Graduate School of Design, and author of *Modern Architecture: Photographs of Ezra Stoller*. He is editor of five books on design.

Michael Sheridan, a former associate research scholar at Columbia University, was project director and a coinvestigator of the New York City Housing Authority study "Defensible Space Evaluated," which was completed in 1998.